PAPIER-MACHE TODAY

SHEILA MᶜGRAW

A FIREFLY BOOK

To Carol and Peter McGraw

A FIREFLY BOOK

Published by Firefly Books Ltd.

Copyright © 1990 Sheila McGraw

Sixth Printing, 2001

Canadian Cataloguing in Publication Data

McGraw, Sheila
Papier-mâché today

ISBN 0-920668-85-2

1. Papier-mâché.   I. Title.

TT871.M24 1990   745.54′2   C90-094515-X

Published in Canada by
Firefly Books Ltd.
3680 Victoria Park Avenue
Willowdale, Ontario M2H 3K1

Published in the United States by
Firefly Books (U.S.) Inc.
P.O. Box 1338, Ellicott Station
Buffalo, New York 14205

Edited by Sarah Swartz, the Editorial Centre
Additional photography by Joy von Tiedemann

Printed and bound in Canada by Friesens, Altona, Manitoba

Acknowledgements
Special thanks to Lionel Koffler for giving me the idea to write this book, and for making the book possible. Also, thanks to all of the people who worked on this project, including Joy von Tiedemann, April Woolner, Paula Ring, Max Piersig, Graham Anthony and Jennifer, Elizabeth and Robbin McGraw, as well as to those who were involved in the book's editing and production.

Contents

Read

Papier-mâché is a medium that fulfills many of the criteria that people desire in a craft. With its wide variety of sculptural treatments and finishing techniques, it satisfies the sculptor, the painter and the craftsperson.

Compared to other art forms, papier-mâché most resembles working with clay, because it is used to build form. This characteristic enables you to add, subtract or alter your papier-mâché object at any stage, giving you the opportunity to make corrections, spontaneous improvements or inspired changes.

Working with papier-mâché allows you a great deal of flexibility. You don't need a huge studio, unless you start making life-sized cows. Nor will you require casting or welding equipment or ovens for firing. You can also work at your own pace. Unless you have a deadline, you can leave your creation for a week or more, and pick up where you left off when you're in the mood.

Papier-mâché is a universal craft, accessible to virtually everyone. Most households have a supply of the basic materials: newspapers, masking tape, flour and water for paste, and some paints.

Children can work in papier-mâché, too, if the project they choose is geared to their level of ability. A common misconception is that papier-mâché is the ideal craft for all children. This has probably been fostered by the fact that the components are inexpensive and, therefore, accessible to kids. In fact, children often find that the application of papier-mâché is tedious or beyond their dexterity, and waiting for objects to dry surpasses their attention span. When planning a project for a child, select something that is medium-sized, simple and relatively speedy. The first project in each of the following sections of this book will meet these criteria and yield impressive results. Remember that a child needs the support and help of an adult to reap the rewards of seeing a project through to completion.

Papier-mâché offers a wide scope for creativity. Your finished object can be naive, sophisticated, humorous, realistic or fantastic. Often the final paint treatment will decide the mood of the finished piece. Objects constructed from papier-mâché can be simple or complex, large or small, easy or ambitious. You can work on a project by yourself or as part of a group. Papier-mâché is incredibly versatile and the choices and ideas are almost limitless.

This First

Introduction

PROPERTIES OF PAPIER-MACHE

Papier-mâché can be pronounced the French way, "papee-ay mashay," or the Anglicized way, "paper mashay." Translated from the French, papier-mâché means, literally, "chewed paper." Those of you who experimented with this medium in grade school probably recall making a pulp of paste and mashed paper bits, then coating balloons or lightbulbs with it to create masks or puppet heads.

While the paper-pulp method still has its uses as a finishing material, it doesn't suit the solid construction of larger items. Most of the projects in this book are medium-to-large figurative objects and feature methods that are easier, stronger, and more appropriate to the building of larger items.

Most projects are done in two stages. The first stage is the construction of an inner structure from chicken wire or densely crumpled, crushed newspaper. Some large objects may also require a wire armature. This inner structure is the general, comprehensive form of the finished object. The second stage consists of covering the structure with layers of papier-mâché and adding more detail to the object.

A papier-mâché object is more ornamental than practical. It will not withstand being left outdoors and it will crack or break if it's handled roughly. Papier-mâché is also flammable, so don't make any candle holders or ashtrays. Unless otherwise stated, the objects in this book are decorative and not intended for practical use.

If you are looking for something fairly quick and simple to make, you should realize that with papier-mâché, small doesn't necessarily mean easy. Often people will set their kids up with a small and intricate project, when in fact something large and simple in shape, like the Bowls project (page 92) is easier, faster, more impressive and altogether more satisfying. Because small is more difficult, I shape items like teeth, nails and eyes from modelling clay rather than forming them from papier-mâché.

On a medium-sized project, larger strips of paper are used, resulting in faster papier-mâché coverage. *Very* large projects require longer construction time and their expansiveness usually involves more coverage in terms of both papier-mâché and painting.

Your first project, even if it is

relatively simple, will take the most time as you become acquainted with the medium. With papier-mâché, as with most other crafts, the more you do, the more confidence you will develop in your skill and in your style, and the faster you will become.

One of the interesting properties of papier-mâché is that it has a mind of its own. Its natural look is uneven and handcrafted. Enjoy this property and don't fight it. You might say that papier-mâché is not an art form for perfectionists. If you want perfectly smooth, symmetrical results, you should investigate another craft, because papier-mâché will drive you crazy!

Keep in mind also that no matter how closely you try to copy a project, it won't be identical to what you see in this book. That is one of the great things about papier-mâché – every piece is an original.

HOW TO USE THIS BOOK

There are five sections in this book. This section, "Read This First," gives general information about materials and construction methods. If you wish to create an original piece of sculpture, all the information that you need is here. Each of the next three sections – "Animals," "Monsters" and "Home Decor" – is comprised of several projects, with specific, detailed instructions for building them. These sections start with a fairly simple project and end with a fairly ambitious one. The projects in-between do not necessarily increase in difficulty. The final section "Finishing," demonstrates various techniques used to decorate and finish the objects.

The time requirements for each project fluctuate, depending on the speed and skill of the person doing the sculpture. Drying times also vary, depending on how wet you mix your paste, how much paste you use and how many layers of paper you apply.

In general, for a medium-sized, not-too-difficult project like the Planter Cat or the Alligator, you should anticipate the following: two or three hours to make the inner structure; two stages of papier-mâché, with a day or more for each stage to dry and a half day for painting and finishing. Allow at least a week for a project, if you are working on it part-time.

The materials and tools you will require are listed at the beginning of each project in the order in which they will be needed. Optional materials are listed separately.

The dimensions of the finished project are also listed. These are approximate and are only meant to give you an idea of the probable results. You can make your projects any size you wish.

Each project features a box for quick reference – "Papier-mâché Basics" – that includes the basic paste recipe and other pertinent information, as well as suggestions for making your work easier.

At the end of most projects, there is a clear photo of the object. This can be used for your reference.

This book is meant to give you ideas and inspiration. Use the instructions as guidelines and create as you go. Feel free to change the details, size and proportions of objects to suit your taste. It's all up to you.

Materials & Equipment

Below is a complete list, in alphabetical order, of the materials and equipment required for papier-mâché construction. Some projects require only the basics of paper and paste. However, some additional tools and materials can make building your object easier and faster and its final appearance more polished.

At the beginning of each project, there is a list of materials required for that specific project. Size, method of construction, and type of finishing will dictate which materials you need and in what quantities you need them.

You probably already have the basic materials for papier-mâché around the house. If not, most of them are easily acquired from hardware, art supply or hobby stores.

BRUSHES:
Choose brushes that correspond to the surface area you are painting… larger square-tipped brushes for large areas, small pointed brushes for detail work etc.

CARDBOARD:
Lightweight or medium-weight cardboard from a cereal box or shoebox may be needed for details. Corrugated cardboard may also be required.

CARPENTER'S GLUE:
Purchase a large jar and add this glue to your paste for extra strength. Carpenter's glue is also available in a small jar with a nozzle, ideal for attaching finishing details.

CHICKEN WIRE:
Purchase lightweight, flexible chicken wire sold by the yard or metre.

FLOUR:
Flour is mixed with water to make paste. Try to purchase the brands that are labelled "easy blending."

FOAM BOARD:
Foam board is a lightweight, non-absorbent alternative to corrugated cardboard. It is available at art and hobby stores.

GLOVES:
Heavy rubber or canvas gloves are needed for handling chicken wire. Thin plastic gloves can protect hands from paste and printer's ink.

HAIR DRYER:
Helps to dry papier-mâché, paint, etc. faster.

HARDWARE ITEMS:
Brackets, screws, nuts and bolts may be needed for mounting sculptures or building an armature.

HOT GLUE GUN:
This appliance is a fast way to apply strong glue for both construction and attaching finishing details. Remember that children should not use a hot glue gun when unsupervised.

JIGSAW:
This saw is used for scroll-cutting plywood when making trays, or for special effects.

KNIVES:
A bread knife may be required for carving papier-mâché; a utility knife for cutting cardboard and other materials is also useful.

MASKING TAPE:
Purchase at least one roll, one inch (2.5 cm) wide. Large projects require wider tape.

MODELLING CLAY:
Purchase commercial modelling clay that bakes hard, or make it yourself. (See recipe, page 142.)

MODELLING PASTE:
A thick plaster-like substance for creating texture or for filling in depressions.

NEWSPAPER:
Newspapers, tabloids or unprinted newsprint can all be used. Several editions of a daily newspaper are enough for most projects.

PAINTS:
Use only acrylic paints for your projects. These are available at art supply stores in premixed colors in tubes and jars.

PAPIER-MACHE PULP:
Available at hobby stores, this can be used as a substitute for modelling clay.

PLASTIC BAGS:
Fit these inside your paste pot for quick cleanup.

PLIERS:
Needle-nose or regular pliers are needed for bending wire. The best kind are those with built-in wire cutters.

PLYWOOD:
Lightweight plywood is necessary for the Trays project and can be used for special effects. Heavier plywood may be needed as a base for sculpture.

POT OR BOWL FOR PASTE:
Use a medium-sized cooking pot or mixing bowl.

PRIMER:
Acrylic primer, also known as gesso, is available in containers of varying size. One medium-sized jar will cover a medium to large project.

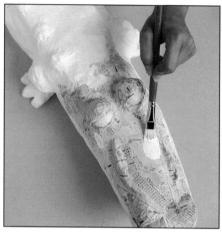

SCISSORS:
Scissors may be needed for cutting string, lightweight cardboard and other materials.

SEWING SUPPLIES:
Fabrics, trim, lace, thread or buttons can be acquired as needed.

STRING:
Butcher string is acceptable when string is required. Nylon fishing line can also be used.

VARNISH:
Glossy or matte acrylic varnish, also known as "medium," is compatible with acrylic paints.

WALLPAPER PASTE:
An alternative to flour and water, a small package of dried wallpaper paste is all that is needed for a large project.

WIRE:
For hanging projects, picture-hanging wire or nylon fishing line is acceptable.

WIRE COAT HANGERS:
Lightweight coat hangers from drycleaners, or wire of similar thickness can be used.

WIRE CUTTERS:
A pair of wire cutters may be necessary for cutting chicken wire and coat hangers.

Getting Started

THE WORK SPACE

Papier-mâché requires some space. You'll need a table or countertop to work on, preferably one that you won't need to clear off frequently. Most of the projects in this book (except for the really large ones) were made on a table about the size of a card table. A card table allows accessibility to the object from all sides, and boxes containing paints and equipment can be stashed underneath it.

Papier-mâché is messy work. If the table doesn't have a plastic top, cover it with a plastic tablecloth, a cut-open garbage bag or a dropsheet for house painting. Don't use newspaper as a protective cover because it will stick to your project as you work on it.

Lighting is very important. If there isn't a light source for your work area, set up a lamp or two and run an extension cord if necessary. Avoid lighting in which you are working in your own shadow.

Although you may do a lot of your papier-mâché standing up, have a chair or stool handy. Bending over a table for a long time can be very hard on your back and neck.

If you are comfortable in your work space, you will have more endurance, be more productive and have a positive attitude about your abilities.

CLEANUP

The best time to think about cleanup is before you start. There are several steps you can take to prevent a major mess that will distract you or slow you down while you are working.

During the construction stage, printer's ink from the newspaper you are using will make your hands very dirty. The ink washes off easily with soap and water, but if you wish to avoid this, purchase thin plastic gloves from drugstores or paint stores.

Before you mix any paste, insert a plastic bag into your paste pot and tape it in place. Mix your paste in it. When you are finished, simply lift out the plastic bag and discard it.

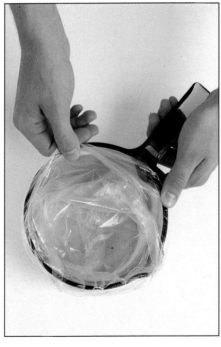

Wear old clothes or an oversized shirt over your clothes to protect them from paste splashes. Paste will come out when clothes are laundered in soap and water, but it won't come out when clothing is drycleaned. Acrylic paints and gesso will not wash out.

If you are working on a large project that overhangs your table, spread a plastic dropsheet on the floor to reduce mopping time or to protect the carpet.

When working with a flour-and-water paste mixture, apply a coat of rich hand cream or Vaseline to your hands before you begin. After working in papier-mâché, soak your hands in warm, soapy water and rub them gently – don't scrub them because they will become sore. You can also purchase thin plastic gloves to avoid wear and tear on your hands.

A neat, orderly work space will make constructing your project more efficient and less frustrating.

NEWSPAPER CONSTRUCTION

For most projects in this book, the construction process begins with an internal structure of geometric shapes made from densely crumpled newspaper wrapped in masking tape. If you are creating an original sculpture, determine which shapes are necessary for the construction of your project by making a sketch or examining a reference photograph. Break the sculpture down into components and note their proportions and relationships.

As you form the component shapes, be sure they are dense and sturdy. Wrap them tightly in masking tape and tape them together securely. Flabby construction at this point will cause problems at the papier-mâché stage.

Here are some guidelines to follow when forming internal geometric shapes.

CONE:
Create a cone by folding several thicknesses of newspaper, as shown in the photo. Tape the overlapping seam closed and trim the uneven, open edge. To make it stay three-dimensional, stuff the cone with newspaper. Cones can be short and wide or long and thin. Adjust your cone shape by tightening or loosening the overlap.

SPHERE:
Crumple a ball of paper. Roll individual sheets of paper over it, keeping the ball tight and dense. Continue rolling single sheets over the sphere until it is the desired size. Wrap it tightly in masking tape.

CYLINDER:
There are two ways to create a cylinder, depending upon the size you want it to be. For a large cylinder, take several layers of newspaper and roll them to form a tube, obtaining the desired diameter. Tape along the seam of the tube. Stuff it with crumpled newspaper. If you want your cylinder to have rounded ends like a sausage, form two balls the diameter of the tube and place them in each end, with crumpled paper packed between them. Tape the balls in place.

For a narrow cylinder, start with a full sheet of newspaper. Working from one end of the sheet to the other, twist the paper tightly. To thicken the cylinder, add extra sheets of paper as you twist. Wrap the cylinder tightly in masking tape.

To keep a cylinder bent or curved, bend it first. Then wrap it in tape while the bend is in place.

CUBE:
If you need a cube shape for a project, construct one from corrugated cardboard or, even better, use an existing box. If any weight is to be placed on it, stuff the cube tightly with crumpled newspaper and tape it shut.

ARMATURES

Occasionally, some projects will need a wire skeleton as well as an inner paper structure. Medium-sized items, like The Mutt (page 38), require a structure of coat hanger wire, while large items like Pigasus (page 74) need a chicken wire form. Your choice of armature will depend on the size, balance and proportion of the finished project, as well as on your personal preference in materials.

The following describes construction methods for armatures and how to use them appropriately.

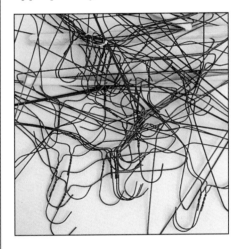

WIRE COAT HANGERS:
Lightweight wire coat hangers from drycleaners or an equivalent thickness of wire purchased from a hardware store can be used. Pliers make the bending of wire far less difficult, although most hangers can be bent and manipulated by hand. They can be cut with wire cutters or broken by bending them in the same place several times. If you acquire pliers that have a built-in wire cutter, they will make your work easier and faster.

Coat hangers are used only as a basic skeleton for containing and supporting the newspaper shapes or as an armature for chicken wire.

SUPPORTS:
A standing figure or similar object requires more support than an object that is low to the ground. To accommodate a project of this type, cut a piece of plywood to an appropriate size. Screw metal brackets to the plywood where the "feet" will be. Choose your brackets to accommodate the size of your figure. They are available in a range of sizes. For large figures you can use the big brackets that are meant for supporting shelving.

Attach wood or metal rods or strapping to the brackets. These will support a chicken wire form. Make this armature as sturdy as possible. (For more information, see Jennifer, page 116.) If assembled and balanced properly, a large dinosaur, a running figure cantilevered from one area on its base, or a large standing figure can all be built in this manner.

CHICKEN WIRE:
Chicken wire is a lightweight mesh, available at hardware outlets and lumberyards, and is sold by the yard or metre. It is very uncomfortable to work with. The sharp, cut ends can scratch and jab you. Always wear heavy rubber or canvas gloves when working with chicken wire (unlike the naughty person in the photos).

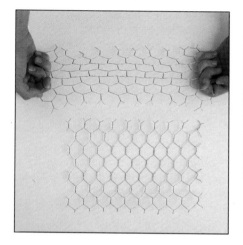

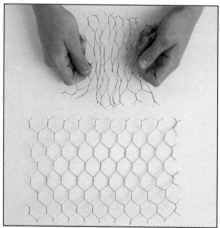

The redeeming quality of this material is its ability to conform and retain the shape that it is molded into. Chicken wire can be stretched and elongated or compressed and shortened. It is also the ideal weight and strength to support the papier-mâché coating applied over it.

MOLDS

Another construction method involves applying papier-mâché over a mold. This is how the Bowls project (page 92) is made.

Papier-mâché is mass-produced using molds constructed from wood, plaster or ceramic. The papier-mâché is layered over the mold and allowed to dry thoroughly. The papier-mâché form is then cut apart, removed from the mold and rejoined by gluing. More papier-mâché is required to cover the join. The result is a very lightweight, thin, hollow finished piece that has subtle definition and accurate symmetry, in contrast with the asymmetrical, individual pieces that are handcrafted.

To produce your own "mass productions," you can use a plastic or china ornament as your mold. Choose one that is inexpensive and simple in shape. You will have to cut apart your papier-mâché to remove it from the mold; the simpler the mold, therefore, the less rejoining you will need to do. A smooth uncluttered shape is best, like a pig, hippo, or a simplified sitting cat.

You can make your own molds from plasticine or plaster of Paris.

Before you start applying the papier-mâché, coat the mold thoroughly with Vaseline. If you miss any areas, the dried papier-mâché will not release and you'll have a very nice mold that's forever covered in papier-mâché! Apply papier-mâché over the mold and allow it to dry. Then cut the shape into quarters and remove it from the mold. Reassemble and papier-mâché over the joins.

The papier-mâché pig shown above was created on a mold. It is hollow and weighs only a few ounces.

Papier-Mâché Application

Paste Recipe

- The basic paste recipe is two parts flour to three parts water.
- Begin with 1 cup (250 mL) of flour, combined with 1½ cups (350 mL) of water.
- Add 2 large spoonfuls of salt. It will help prevent mold forming in your paste or on your project.
- The paste should have the consistency of cream of mushroom soup without the mushrooms.
- Add more flour to thicken, or more water to thin the mixture.
- This quantity will last for about two hours of papier-mâché application.
- Carpenter's glue, about ¼ cup (50 mL), can be added to the paste for extra strength.

Once your internal construction has been formed, papier-mâché is applied over the exterior. Here is a list and discussion of the necessary steps and components for applying the papier-mâché.

NEWSPAPER:
Papier-mâché is the most enjoyable way to recycle your newspapers. Accumulate several editions of your daily paper before you begin. Newspaper is necessary for two stages of your project. The first stage is the inner paper construction. The second is the application of papier-mâché.

When you have completed your paper construction, tear a supply of newspaper strips, about two inches (5 cm) wide. *Newspaper has a grain. Tear it one way and it's a mess; tear it the other way, however, and it tears straight.*

PAPIER-MACHE PASTE:
The next step is to mix your paste. Select a medium-sized mixing bowl or pot. Avoid using a flat pan, since a large surface area will permit the paste to thicken or dry while you are still working. Place a plastic bag inside your paste pot for easier cleanup.

WALLPAPER PASTE:
Wallpaper paste can be used instead of flour-and-water paste and it has several advantages. It lasts in the pot far longer without rotting, it allows a smoother application of papier-mâché and it washes very easily from your hands. However, it isn't as strong as flour-and-water paste and most people don't have a box of it on their kitchen shelves, whereas they usually do have flour available.

A small box of dried wallpaper paste is more than enough for a medium to large project. To mix the paste, ignore the instructions on the box, which are for large quantities. Instead, add the dry paste, a pinch at a time, to about 2 cups (500 mL) of *warm* water, mixing it constantly with your hands to eliminate all lumps. When the consistency is like heavy cream, allow the paste to sit for 15 minutes. It will thicken slightly in this period.

GENERAL APPLICATION:

Begin your papier-mâché by smearing paste over a section of your project. Get it good and wet. One by one, lay strips of newspaper onto the wet-paste area and smooth them down with more paste. Do not dip them into the paste first.

Continue adding and overlapping strips of paper and more paste until you have accumulated at least three layers. (Five layers are preferable.) The more layers of papier-mâché you apply, the stronger your creation will be.

When applying the newspaper strips, alternate the direction, vertically for the first layer, horizontally for the second layer, and so on. This will avoid the creation of weak spots from strips piled directly on top of each other. It will also give you an even coverage. Don't feel you must use long strips of paper. Tear them off to whatever length best fits the area on which you are working.

TRICKY AREAS:

On nearly every project, there is an area of papier-mâché that consists of small indentations, hills and valleys or rounded shapes to which the paper won't easily adhere or conform.

To tackle these areas effectively, the first consideration is stability. Be certain that there are no moving parts. Using masking tape, secure the area well and make sure that taped-together pieces are firm. If tape alone won't do the job, you can tie pieces together with string or fishing line. The string can be covered with papier-mâché and, when your form is dry, any excess string can be cut away.

When working over intricate and rounded areas, use narrower newspaper strips than usual. A half-inch (1.25 cm) width is about right. You can also try tearing into the sides of the paper strips. This allows the strip to be curved, with the torn pieces fanning out on one side and overlapping themselves on the other.

Layering the strips at right angles to each other helps to reinforce pieces and hold down stray ends.

CHICKEN WIRE:

To encourage paper strips to adhere to chicken wire, apply random strips of masking tape to the mesh. Then, for the first layer of papier-mâché, dip the newspaper strips in the paste *before* applying them. Once you have applied the first layer, proceed according to "General Application," section.

THE DRYING PROCESS:

Allow the papier-mâché to dry thoroughly before moving on to the finishing stage of your project. Placing the item on a heat register, in a sunny location or in an oven at *low temperature* can speed up the drying time, as will the air from a fan or hair dryer. If your project feels cool to the touch, it is still damp and requires more drying time.

If your project is large or if you place it on plastic to dry, it may develop mold or mildew in the areas where it contacts a surface. To avoid this, rotate the item or place it where it will have complete air circulation around it.

When the papier-mâché is completely dry, it can be primed and finished in whatever ways you like. (See FINISHING section for ideas.)

The purpose of this book is to have fun. If something isn't evolving exactly as it appears in the book, don't get frustrated. Change and adapt the project to fit what's happening. Most errors can be turned to your advantage. Don't forget – at any point in the construction, you can add, subtract or change it. In fact, some of the best pieces have resulted from happenstance. It's all part of the creative process of this wonderful craft.

Animals

T he animals featured in this section are caricatures of the real thing. Some, like Meatloaf Cat, Alligator and Birdo, are extreme parodies or cartoons. This is partly for fun, but also, in the case of Meatloaf Cat and Alligator, to simplify the construction. The design and patterns of the finishing paint job and the choice of colors enhance the cartoon effect. With other projects, such as The Mutt and the Planter Cat, the animals are created in fairly realistic sizes and finishes to tease the viewer. The viewer might do a double take and mistake your animal for a real one – but only for an instant. The animals created from papier-mâché should always be disarmingly unreal. These aren't those five-and-dime, plaster and paint collie dogs or Persian cats, masquerading as the genuine article.

Before you start your animal, always draw a sketch or find a picture for reference. If you want to make a cartoon animal, a sketch is best. When working from a photo, most people get bogged down in realism and try to match the photo. A sketch allows you to keep your original goals in mind. Conversely, a photo will help those who are looking for realistic details or proportions. These reference pictures will help keep you on track throughout your project. No matter how crude some of my sketches have been, I always refer to them during the construction stages of a project.

Many animals have body shapes that lend themselves to papier-mâché construction. The hippo, walrus, penguin and elephant are just a few. Use the instructions as guidelines for creating other animals. Most can be made from an inner construction of formed newspaper or a combination of coat hanger wire and newspaper. Medium to large animals can be formed from chicken wire. (See pages 15 and 17, for more information on chicken wire construction.) Once a firm internal structure has been formed, papier-mâché is applied to the outside and allowed to dry. Finally, the animal is painted and finishing items like teeth and toenails can be added.

Create a menagerie of pets: guard dogs or lapdogs, poodles, bulldogs or basset hounds, cozy cats that occupy a hearth or a windowsill, or birds that hang from the ceiling or nest in a corner. Install a zoo of exotic creatures in your house: an alligator for the bathroom, a hippo for the kitchen and a giant bird for the nursery or den.

Sleeping cats recline in interesting positions: the crescent roll, the chicken, and, my favorite, the meatloaf. The meatloaf position lends itself well to papier-mâché, because it is low to the ground and streamlined. This cat is purposely simplified, but its paint job can animate it and give it lots of personality. (For a more traditional and ambitious cat, see the Planter Cat, page 32.)

This Meatloaf Cat is made from easy components, mainly cylinders and balls made from crumpled and rolled newspapers. The components are taped solidly together before you apply the papier-mâché. The more complete and sturdy you make your animal's inner construction, the less work you'll have during the papier-mâché stage. If your proportions don't conform to what's shown here, don't worry. This cat can be long and thin or short and round. The head can be large or small.

Once your basic structure is made, you can still change it. Before you apply the papier-mâché, you can modify your construction or even add some new pieces. This cat's appeal is its wild and crazy cartoon appearance.

Meatloaf Cat

How to do it

MATERIALS:
Newspaper
Masking tape
Flour and water
Lightweight cardboard
Utility knife
Primer (gesso)
Acrylic paints and brushes

OPTIONAL:
String
Carpenter's glue for paste
Varnish

FINISHED SIZE:
Length: 11 inches (28 cm)
(excluding tail)
Width: 6¼ inches (16 cm)

1 To form the cat's body, roll and tape a tube made from about five layers of newspaper. Trim or add to the tube, if necessary, to make it about twice as long as it is wide. Tape the tube closed.

2 Make two balls of crumpled newspaper. Wrap each ball in tape so that each one is solid. These balls should be large enough to fit snugly in each end of the tube.

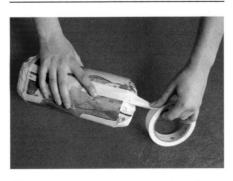

3 Place one ball in one end of the tube. Tape it in place. Stuff the tube with newspaper. Tape the other ball into the other end. The tube should now look like a large, fat sausage.

4 Make two flat balls of crumpled paper for haunches. Wrap each ball in tape. Put the balls aside for now.

5 To make the front legs and tail, form lengths of twisted newspaper. Wrap them in tape, then cut them to the desired lengths. Put these aside for now.

6 Form a ball of tightly crumpled paper for the head. Wrap it in tape. It can be as round or as flat as you like. Put this aside also.

7 Position and tape the haunches to the sides of the body like earmuffs. If the haunches won't stay close to the body, tie them in place with string.

Position and tape the tail and the front legs in place on the underside of the body. The head will be attached later.

8 Cut triangle-shaped ears, each with a rounded tip, from lightweight cardboard. Make a V-shaped cut into the base of each ear. Pull the sections together to close the gap and tape it shut. This will give the ears some dimension.

Position the ears on the head and tape them in place.

9 Tear strips of newspaper and mix your flour-and-water paste. (See box.)

Apply paste onto a section of your cat-to-be. One by one, lay strips of newspaper on the wet section, smoothing each strip down with more paste.

Progress over the entire structure of your cat. Papier-mâché over any string that is in contact with the body. Cover the cat with at least three layers of papier-mâché.

While the cat's body is drying, papier-mâché the head. Let everything dry.

10 Cut away any excess, exposed string.

Using a utility knife, cut a shallow hole in the body to set the head into, starting small and making it bigger if necessary.

Papier-mâché Basics

NEWSPAPER STRIPS
- Newspaper has a grain. Tear it in the right direction and it will tear straight and evenly.

CLEANUP
- Place a plastic bag in your paste pot for quick cleanup.
- Coat your hands with Vaseline for easier paste removal.

PASTE RECIPE
- Add 1½ cups (350 mL) water to 1 cup (250 mL) flour. Mix it with your hands.
- Add 2 large spoonfuls of salt. Salt will help prevent mold from forming in your paste or on your project.
- Add about ¼ cup (50 mL) of carpenter's glue for extra strength (optional).

APPLICATION
- When spreading paste, apply it liberally.
- Do not dip the paper strips in the paste. Lay each strip on the wet paste area and smooth over with more paste.
- Apply at least three layers. Five is preferable.

DRYING
- Papier-mâché can take more than one day to dry.
- Test your project by touch. If it feels cool, it needs more time to dry.

11 Tape the head in place. Before wetting the area with papier-mâché paste, be sure the head is taped securely. This is the trickiest part. If the head is wobbly, it will be difficult to attach. If necessary, tie the head in position with string.

Papier-mâché the head to the body, covering all tape and any string that is in contact with the area. Let it dry thoroughly.

12 Prime your cat with gesso, a white acrylic primer that will prevent the newsprint from showing through your paint.

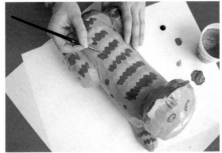

13 Using acrylic paints, paint your cat any color or design you want. It can be traditional or crazy – it's up to you. (See FINISHING section for ideas.)

14 A final coat of acrylic varnish, either flat or glossy, will add durability to your creation.

15 Place your cat on a window sill for pigeon perusal.

Alligator

Low to the ground and cylindrical in shape, the crocodile or alligator is ideal for papier-mâché. The reptile featured here has some lovable qualities that the real creature lacks. It is bright and comical-looking, it won't creep out of your bathtub and it won't eat you.

The only tricky parts of the construction are the legs and the feet and the application of papier-mâché around them. Otherwise, building the beast is straightforward and the papier-mâché work is reasonably speedy on the large areas.

The animal's inner structure is made from crumpled and rolled newspaper. Be sure to keep this as dense and sturdy as possible and tape all of your paper construction well. This will strengthen your alligator and prevent soft spots in the papier-mâché. Finishing details make this alligator fun and interesting: eyes, teeth and bumps along its back.

When finished, this is a good-sized, humorous creature suitable for a child's room, a bathroom or as a living room conversation piece.

How to do it

MATERIALS:
Newspaper
Masking tape
String
Flour and water
Lightweight cardboard
Utility knife
Primer (gesso)
Acrylic paints and brushes

OPTIONAL:
Carpenter's glue for paste
Modelling clay or commercial
   papier-mâché pulp
Hot glue or carpenter's glue

FINISHED SIZE:
Length: 36 inches (91.5 cm)
Width: 5½ inches (14 cm)
     (not including legs)

1 To form the alligator's body, make a long cone from four or five layers of newspaper. Tape the cone shut. This cone will be about two-thirds of the finished length of the alligator. The head will make up the other third.

  Stuff the cone with crumpled newspaper. Make it quite solid.

2 Like the real thing, this alligator's head is mainly mouth. Make two slightly flat, oblong shapes, one for the top jaw and one for the bottom. Make these about half the length of the body. The bottom jaw should be a little shorter and narrower than the top one.

  Wrap each jaw in tape.

3 Align the jaws at one end and tape them together securely. They should remain slightly open at the untaped end.

4 To create the legs, make two long cylinders from tightly twisted, full sheets of newspaper. Wrap each cylinder in tape.

5 Place the cylinders across the alligator's body. They should extend on both sides. Tape them in place on the alligator's back. Bend the cylinders down, and don't worry if they stick out at the sides.

  Tape the jaws securely to the wide end of the cone-shaped body.

6 Add crumpled newspaper to the alligator's body to give it some bulk. Tape it down as you go. You can fatten the stomach and fill in the area where the head is attached to the body. Add some paper to the back to fill in between the leg pieces. Wrap the whole body in tape, so that it is solid and sturdy.

8 Turn your alligator upside down. Bend the cylinders to make them look more like alligator legs. Loop string around each pair of legs from side to side. To keep the legs close to the body, pull the string tight and tie it. Turn the alligator rightside up and adjust the shape of the legs.

Trim the legs if they are too long. If you prefer your alligator with legs that stick out, trim them to the appropriate length and leave them untied. Toes will be added later.

Papier-mâché around the legs, covering string where it is in contact with the legs. Allow the area to dry.

7 Tear your newspaper strips and mix your flour-and-water paste. (See box.)

Start by covering a good-sized area of the head or body with paste. One by one, lay strips of paper over the paste-covered area and smooth down the strips with more paste. Apply at least three layers of papier-mâché.

Papier-mâché the alligator's body and head. Do not papier-mâché the legs. They will be done later. Allow it to dry.

9 Cut away any excess, exposed string.

Cut four feet (with toes attached), from lightweight cardboard. Tape them to the ends of the legs. When the alligator is placed upright on a flat surface, the feet should stay flat. Add crumpled newspaper to the tops of the toes and feet. Wrap them in tape.

Papier-mâché around the toes and feet and onto the legs for reinforcement.

Papier-mâché Basics

NEWSPAPER STRIPS
- **Newspaper has a grain. Tear it in the right direction and it will tear straight and evenly.**

CLEANUP
- **Place a plastic bag in your paste pot for quick cleanup.**
- **Coat your hands with Vaseline for easier paste removal.**

PASTE RECIPE
- **Add 1½ cups (350 mL) water to 1 cup (250 mL) flour. Mix it with your hands.**
- **Add 2 large spoonfuls of salt. Salt will help prevent mold from forming in your paste or on your project.**
- **Add about ¼ cup (50 mL) of carpenter's glue for extra strength (optional).**

APPLICATION
- **When spreading paste, apply it liberally.**
- **Do not dip the paper strips in the paste. Lay each strip on the wet paste area and smooth over with more paste.**
- **Apply at least three layers. Five is preferable.**

DRYING
- **Papier-mâché can take more than one day to dry.**
- **Test your project by touch. If it feels cool, it needs more time to dry.**

10 Examine your reptile to decide whether you want bumps on its back. These go in two rows from the front of the snout to the tip of the tail. Make the bumps from small wads of crumpled newspaper dipped in flour-and-water paste. Position the bumps and papier-mâché over them, using narrow strips of paper.

11 Form the toenails, eyes, teeth and tongue from papier-mâché, modelling clay (see FINISHING section, page 142) or from the papier-mâché pulp available at hobby stores. Paint them and set all but the eyes aside for the moment.

12 Using hot glue or carpenter's glue, attach the eyes.
Form the eyelids with papier-mâché. Let these dry.

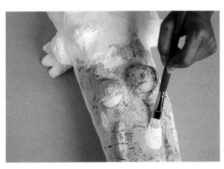

13 Prime the alligator with gesso, a white acrylic primer that will prevent the newsprint from showing through your paint.

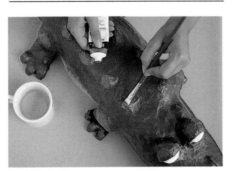

14 Using acrylic paints, paint your reptile the green of your choice. To emphasize the bumps, paint their tops a lighter green, blending it in.

15 Attach the tongue, toenails and teeth with hot glue or carpenter's glue. The toenails and teeth will be more secure if you cut small holes into the papier-mâché with a utility knife and glue the parts into the holes. Tape them in place until the glue is dry.

16 Place your alligator beside the bathtub to snap at little pink toes.

Planter Cat

O ne of the things that cats do best is to relax in poses that are both economical and sensual. The way in which sleeping cats curl themselves up and tuck everything under so neatly makes them ideal papier-mâché subjects. I got my inspiration for the Planter Cat from watching my cat Clawdia sleep.

The simple basic shapes that make up the Planter Cat's internal structure ensure an almost foolproof project. However, this cat can be somewhat time-consuming to make because it requires several stages of papier-mâché and the accompanying drying times. Some of the papier-mâché is intricate because small indentations and hills and valleys are created around the cat's legs and tail where they join the body.

The structure also requires estimating proportions. At the outset, make a small reference sketch or find a photo of a cat to help you with proportions and relationships among body parts.

This cat is of a fairly realistic size. It lends itself well to different finishes like calico designs, traditional cat markings or whimsical découpage decorations. (See FINISHING section for ideas.) Because of its realism and true-to-life proportions, your Planter Cat will impress admirers and surprise the unsuspecting.

Whether to make this cat into a planter or not is optional. I thought the idea of a planter nicely complemented the country feeling of this cat.

How to do it

MATERIALS:
Newspaper
Masking tape
Flour and water
Lightweight cardboard
Scissors
Utility knife
Primer (gesso)
Acrylic paints and brushes

OPTIONAL:
String
Carpenter's glue for paste
Bread knife
Clay or plastic flower pot
Varnish
Plastic bag
Plant or flowers

FINISHED SIZE:
Length: 12 inches (30.5 cm)
(excluding tail)
Width: 9 inches (23 cm)

1 To make the cat's body, crumple several sheets of newspaper over each other until you have a slightly flat ball, about the size of a large grapefruit. Roll the ball tightly so that it is dense and sturdy.

2 Tightly wrap the body-ball in masking tape to retain its shape.

3 Make three smaller balls, one for the chest and two flatter ones for the haunches. Mash the two haunches with the palm of your hand to make them flat if they are too round. Wrap all the balls tightly in masking tape.

4 Tape the round and flat balls to the body in the appropriate places: the round chest-ball on the front of the body and the two flat balls on each side like earmuffs. Be sure to attach all the balls securely.

If necessary, tie string around the haunches so they do not pull away from the body. The excess string will be cut away after the papier-mâché application.

Place your cat's body on a flat surface and check its balance.

5 While you're in a ball-making mood, make and tape a *slightly* pointed ball for the cat's head and set it aside.

For the legs and tail, make three cylinders. Twist a full sheet of newspaper for each cylinder. Bend each cylinder in half and twist again. Wrap masking tape securely around each cylinder. To make a curved cylinder, shape it before taping.

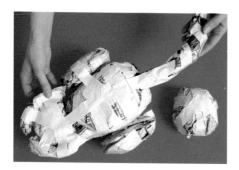

6 Attach the front legs and tail to the underside of the body in the appropriate positions. They can be curved or straight.

If the legs pull away from the body, or if the tail won't stay curved, tie them into position with string. The head will be attached later.

7 Tear your strips of newspaper and mix your flour-and-water paste. (See box.)

Work in sections. Apply paste over a large section of your cat (top or bottom). Take strips of newspaper, one at a time. Lay them directly onto the section of the body that has paste on it and smooth them down with more paste. Continue laying overlapping strips of paper as you progress over the entire structure until it is covered with at least three layers of papier-mâché.

8 While the papier-mâché is drying, cut out two triangle-shaped cardboard ears, each with a rounded tip. Make a V-shaped cut into the base of each ear. Pull the sections together to close the gap and tape it shut. This will give the ears some dimension. Position them on the head and tape them in place.

9 After the body of your headless cat has dried, cut out a shallow hole with a utility knife and set the head into it. Tape it in position. Adjust the ears if necessary.

10 Attach the head to the body with papier-mâché, covering any tape.

Papier-mâché Basics

NEWSPAPER STRIPS
- Newspaper has a grain. Tear it in the right direction and it will tear straight and evenly.

CLEANUP
- Place a plastic bag in your paste pot for quick cleanup.
- Coat your hands with Vaseline for easier paste removal.

PASTE RECIPE
- Add 1½ cups (350 mL) water to 1 cup (250 mL) flour. Mix it with your hands.
- Add 2 large spoonfuls of salt. Salt will help prevent mold from forming in your paste or on your project.
- Add about ¼ cup (50 mL) of carpenter's glue for extra strength (optional).

APPLICATION
- When spreading paste, apply it liberally.
- Do not dip the paper strips in the paste. Lay each strip on the wet paste area and smooth over with more paste.
- Apply at least three layers. Five is preferable.

DRYING
- Papier-mâché can take more than one day to dry.
- Test your project by touch. If it feels cool, it needs more time to dry.

11 Examine your cat and see if you like its shape. If not, now is the time to fix it. You can add details like a nose and whisker pads and fill in depressions or areas that are too flat by adding crumpled paper dipped in paste. Parts that protrude can be trimmed away with a bread knife. The long blade of the bread knife provides better control than a utility knife. Papier-mâché over any corrections.

If you do not want to make a planter out of your cat, skip to step 16.

12 OPTIONAL: Place a flower pot upside down on the cat's back and trace around it.

13 OPTIONAL: Cut along your traced outline and remove the circle of papier-mâché. Keep cutting and digging out the paper interior until your flower pot fits comfortably inside. The hole should be slightly larger than the pot.

14 OPTIONAL: Press the edges of the hole to compress the paper inside. Tape the edges and test the fit of your flower pot. Remove the pot.

15 OPTIONAL: Papier-mâché over the inside of the hole. Let it dry.

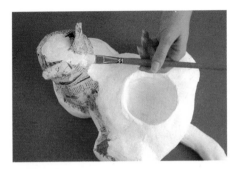

16 When your cat has dried thoroughly, prime the whole creature with gesso, a white acrylic primer that will prevent newsprint from showing through your paint.

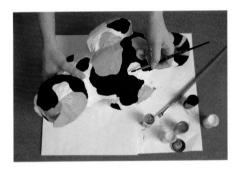

17 Using acrylic paints, paint your cat any color or design you wish. (See FINISHING section for ideas.)

18 A clear varnish can be applied for durability. If you have made a planter, seal and waterproof the flower-pot hole by applying at least two generous coats of acrylic medium varnish. You may also wish to insert a small plastic bag into the cavity before setting your plant or flowers inside.

The Mutt

Dogs come in a multitude of sizes and shapes. There are chubby, skinny, goofy, fierce and friendly ones. Browsing through a book on dogs or observing dogs in the park can help you decide which kind of dog you would like to make. Avoid fluffy ones. They are best made as plush toys, unless you are prepared to attach hair to your finished papier-mâché pet.

The dog featured here has been named Bartholomew, after the real dog that spontaneously approached and sniffed him while we were taking photographs in the park. Our Bartholomew is a basic mutt, unlike his namesake, who is a purebred basset hound. Bartholomew is definitely overweight and holds no pedigree, but he's quiet and won't pester you to take him for a walk. His food bills are also extremely low.

Don't be intimidated by this dog. Although quite large, it has fairly simple components and you end up with a very impressive, good-sized project. To assess the proportions, make a rough sketch or find a picture of the type of dog you wish to make. I have found, time and again, that when you're in the midst of construction it's easy to lose sight of your original goals. A reference sketch or photo will help keep you on track.

The instructions are for a rather tube-like dog. If you prefer a shapely dog like a bulldog, boxer or Doberman pinscher, refer to the instructions highlighted as ALTERNATIVE as well as the instructions for the regular dog. There are several drying times involved in the building of Bartholomew and a good deal of papier-mâché is required. But perseverance and patience will pay off.

A lot of the character and the breed of your dog will show in the paint job, which can be as simple, complicated or abstract as you like. (See FINISHING section for ideas.)

When your dog is finished, you can test the premise that people choose dogs that resemble their owners.

How to do it

MATERIALS:

5 wire coat hangers

Newspaper

Masking tape

Flour and water

Medium-weight cardboard

Scissors

Pliers or wire cutters

Primer (gesso)

Acrylic paints and brushes

OPTIONAL:

Pliers

Carpenter's glue for paste

2 black buttons for eyes

Hot glue, or carpenter's glue

Dog collar and leash

FINISHED SIZE:

Length: 27 inches (68.5 cm)
(from nose to tail)

Width: 10 inches (25.5 cm)
(across hips)

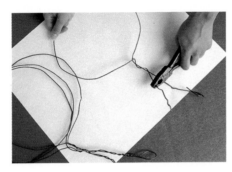

1 Untwist and straighten five wire coat hangers with pliers or by hand. Using four of them, form hoops about the diameter you'd like your dog's body to be. Twist the end of the wire to secure the hoop. These wires will resemble the letter "q." The downstrokes of the "q" shape will be the dog's legs. Bend the hook-ends of the hangers closed. These will be the feet.

For a shapely dog, unlike Bartholomew, follow ALTERNATIVE steps until you reach step 10.

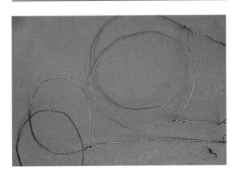

2 ALTERNATIVE: If you want your dog's chest to be larger than its hips, make the two chest-hoops larger in diameter than the other two hoops. This will make the leg-wires longer on the small hoops. Do not trim them.

3 For the chest and the rear end, crumple two balls of newspaper. Keep rolling more and more layers of paper tightly over each ball until they are the right size to fit tightly into the hoops. Wrap the balls in masking tape.

4 ALTERNATIVE: Make one paper ball the correct size of the chest-hoops and one smaller ball to fit the hip-hoops.

5 Place two hoops together around each paper ball with the legs on opposite sides. Wrap the balls and hoops in tape.

6 To make the dog's body, use six or eight sheets of newspaper to roll a tube having the diameter of the paper balls. Tape the tube shut.

7 Place a paper ball into one end of the tube. Pack the center of the tube with crumpled paper and place the other paper ball in the open end. Tape all of the parts together. Be sure the tube is well packed and the body is quite solid. Flabby construction will give you problems later on during the papier-mâché stage.

At this point, you can set your dog up to see if he stands evenly and if his shape is correct. This is when you can make your dog shorter, longer, fatter or thinner. The way he looks now will determine how he will look later.

8 ALTERNATIVE: Proceed as in step 7, making the paper tube the diameter of the largest (chest) ball. When the balls are in place, turn your dog over onto its back. Slash into the end of the tube, making several cuts as far as the chest. Do this starting from the rear end, on the underside (belly) only.

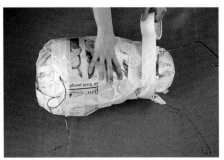

9 ALTERNATIVE: Wrap the tube in masking tape, pulling the cut sections tight to conform to the size of the small hips.

Stand your dog up. Position the legs and cut the rear ones or add more wire to the front ones so that the dog's back is level. Form hooks at the ends of the wires for feet.

10 To form the neck, make a cone from four or five layers of newspaper. Test it on your dog's body. Trim the length and adjust the width to fit. Cut slashes into the widest part of the cone shape if necessary.

Stuff the cone tightly with crumpled newspaper. Tape it securely in place on the body.

11 For haunches, crumple and form newspaper into two pork chop shapes. Wrap them in tape.

Position them on the hind legs and body of the dog. Tape them in place.

Papier-mâché Basics

NEWSPAPER STRIPS

- Newspaper has a grain. Tear it in the right direction and it will tear straight and evenly.

CLEANUP

- Place a plastic bag in your paste pot for quick cleanup.
- Coat your hands with Vaseline for easier paste removal.

PASTE RECIPE

- Add 1½ cups (350 mL) water to 1 cup (250 mL) flour. Mix it with your hands.
- Add 2 large spoonfuls of salt. Salt will help prevent mold from forming in your paste or on your project.
- Add about ¼ cup (50 mL) of carpenter's glue for extra strength (optional).

APPLICATION

- When spreading paste, apply it liberally.
- Do not dip the paper strips in the paste. Lay each strip on the wet paste area and smooth over with more paste.
- Apply at least three layers. Five is preferable.

DRYING

- Papier-mâché can take more than one day to dry.
- Test your project by touch. If it feels cool, it needs more time to dry.

12 Wrap twisted paper around the exposed coat hangers to shape and fatten up the legs. Tape well.

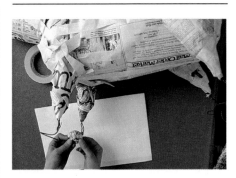

13 Bend the closed hooks at the ends of the legs so they are at right angles to the legs (all facing forward, of course). Form the paws by jamming balls of paper into the closed hooks. Wrap them in tape.

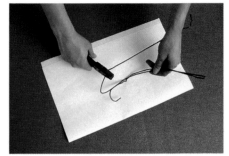

14 Bend the last coat hanger in half. Determine the length you'd like the tail to be. Then bend the excess wire to each side to form two hooks, approximately three inches long. Cut off the excess wire, using pliers or wire cutters.

15 Attach the tail to the body by sliding the two hooks under the top-center of the back hoop.

16 Bend the tail the way you'd like it to be: up, down, curly or straight. Wrap twisted paper around the tail, making it thick at the base and tapering toward the end. Tape the tail securely. You now have a headless dog shape.

17 Now it's time to start the papier-mâché. Tear your strips of newspaper and mix your flour-and-water paste. (See box.)

Apply paste over a section of your dog-to-be. One by one, lay newspaper strips on the paste-covered section and smooth them down with more paste. Progress over the dog's body until the entire beast is covered with at least three layers of papier-mâché. Allow it to dry.

19 Cut the ears and tongue (optional) from medium-weight cardboard. Make a V-shaped cut into the base of each ear. Pull the sections together to close the gap and tape it shut. This will give the ears some dimension. Bend both ears for a look of playfulness, bend one ear for a look of anticipation, or leave both ears up for an alert look.

The tongue can also be cut, shaped and bent.

21 Your dog's face is now quite pointed, which is fine for some breeds. If you wish to plump out the face of wondermutt, you can do so by adding folded and crumpled paper for a brow, whisker pads and a bottom jaw, taping as you go. The tongue should also be added now.

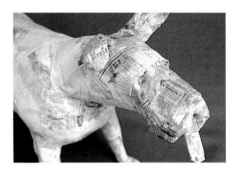

18 Now that you can better visualize your dog, you can begin to make his head. Form and tape shut a cone made from rolled newspaper. Trim and slash the sides so that it fits onto the dog's neck and stuff it tightly with crumpled newspaper.

20 Position the head, then stand back and examine your dog. Adjust the size and position of the head if necessary and tape it securely in place. Then tape the ears in place.

22 Papier-mâché the head and neck. If you like, build up certain areas with crumpled paper dipped in paste and papier-mâché over these areas. You can also thicken the ears and the tongue. Let the dog dry completely.

23 Prime your dog with gesso, a white acrylic primer that will prevent newsprint from showing through your paint.

25 OPTIONAL: For the dog's eyes, secure buttons in place with hot glue or carpenter's glue. Attach a dog collar and a leash for an extra note of realism.

24 When the primer is dry, you can paint your dog however you wish. If you opt for realism, remember that all dogs are either black, white, ginger or brown shades. A realistic paint job needn't be complicated. A solid tan dog, or a graphically spotted dalmation can be very effective. (See FINISHING section for more details.)

26 OPTIONAL: Apply a coat of matte varnish to your dog's body for extra protection. Gloss varnish can add a wet look to nose and mouth.

27 Position your dog at patio doors to scare off intruders.

Birdo

This bird escaped from its natural habitat – the papier-mâché jungles of South America – to roost in your living room or nursery. Please be prepared to help out with the babies when the eggs hatch.

Most people who see Birdo want to own her. It must have something to do with her size and bulk, or her hairdo, or just her resigned expression. Parents seem to identify with her the most.

Birdo *is* quite large. You can scale her down if you wish. She's great as an ornament for an empty corner or to add a dash of color to a room. Remember that Birdo is ornamental and not strong enough for children to climb on.

This project is the largest and most ambitious of the Animal projects, requiring an inner structure made from coat hangers, densely crumpled newspaper and lots of masking tape. The body structure can be formed from chicken wire instead of newspaper and masking tape, if you prefer. (See pages 15 and 17, for more information on chicken wire construction.) This bird is too large to be built on a table. The most convenient place to work is the floor, which means you will bend and stretch a lot.

The papier-mâché for this project is time-consuming because there is a large area to cover and it must be done in stages. There are several drying times involved.

Any bird made according to these instructions is not going to look exactly like Birdo because there are so many variables. Be prepared to fashion your own unique creature as you progress.

How to do it

MATERIALS:

12 wire coat hangers

Pliers or wire cutters

Newspaper

Masking tape

String

Utility knife

Flour and water

Medium-weight cardboard

Primer (gesso)

Acrylic paints and brushes

Carpenter's glue or hot glue

OPTIONAL:

Carpenter's glue for paste

Commercial modelling clay or
    papier-mâché pulp

Finishing items

FINISHED SIZE:

Length: 32 inches (81 cm)
        (to top of head)

Width: 24 inches (61 cm)

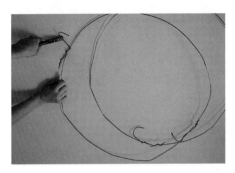

1 To form the bird's body, use pliers to untwist and straighten four wire coat hangers. Twist the ends of two wires together to create one long wire. Form it into a large oval shape, twisting the ends shut. Do this with the other two wires. You should now have two wire ovals.

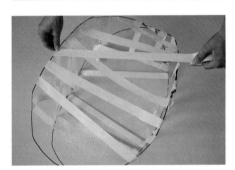

2 Place the ovals inside each other at right angles. Wrap them loosely with masking tape to form a large, three-dimensional oval. Leave one end untaped for stuffing.

3 Turn the oval on its taped end and stuff crumpled newspaper into the cavity until it is completely full. Continue taping around the outside and stuffing the inside until you have a pleasing body shape for your bird. The paper stuffing should be fairly dense and the tape should be tight.

4 Stretch out five wire coat hangers, four for the legs and one for the neck. Do not untwist them or straighten the hooks.

Hook one stretched-out coat hanger onto each side wire of the body frame. Squeeze the hooks tightly closed with pliers.

For the neck, hook one stretched-out coat hanger onto the front where the wires of the body frame intersect. Tighten this hook too.

5 Tape all the coat hanger wires for the legs and neck in position against the body to help strengthen the structure.

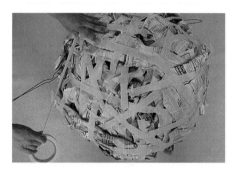

6 To pad the bird's body and prevent the coat hangers from making ridges in your papier-mâché, crumple newspaper and tape it over the bird's body. Pack the body solidly.

7 Wrap twisted newspaper around the tops of the legs. Wrap them securely in tape.

Hook two stretched-out coat hangers into the ends of the existing legs and tighten the hooks with pliers.

8 To keep the legs from sliding apart, untwist and straighten a coat hanger and cut it to span Birdo's stomach, using pliers or wire cutters. Hook one end around each leg. Tighten the hooks with pliers.

9 Continue twisting paper around the legs, building it up for knobby knees. Stop about two-thirds of the way down the drumsticks. Wrap the legs in tape.

10 Make three or four eggs by rolling crumpled newspaper in more and more layers. Wrap tape around each egg. The egg-balls should be dense and sturdy, since Birdo will want to sit on them.

11 Bend up the uncovered end of each coat hanger to form the center toe.

Place your bird on several eggs to see how she sits. Adjust the sizes of the eggs, if necessary, to make her comfortable and stable.

12 Crumple paper to form two pork chop shapes for the wings. Wrap them in tape.

Tape the wings in place. Reinforce them by tying string around the bird.

Papier-mâché Basics

NEWSPAPER STRIPS
- Newspaper has a grain. Tear it in the right direction and it will tear straight and evenly.

CLEANUP
- Place a plastic bag in your paste pot for quick cleanup.
- Coat your hands with Vaseline for easier paste removal.

PASTE RECIPE
- Add 1½ cups (350 mL) water to 1 cup (250 mL) flour. Mix it with your hands.
- Add 2 large spoonfuls of salt. Salt will help prevent mold from forming in your paste or on your project.
- Add about ¼ cup (50 mL) of carpenter's glue for extra strength (optional).

APPLICATION
- When spreading paste, apply it liberally.
- Do not dip the paper strips in the paste. Lay each strip on the wet paste area and smooth over with more paste.
- Apply at least three layers. Five is preferable.

DRYING
- Papier-mâché can take more than one day to dry.
- Test your project by touch. If it feels cool, it needs more time to dry.

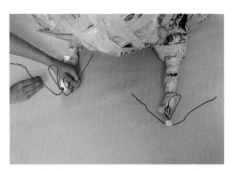

13 Form two additional toes on each foot by twisting coat hanger wire around the base of the existing toe. Allow wire to extend on either side of the middle toe. Cut the wire to the desired length, using pliers or wire cutters. Tape around the intersection of the wires.

14 Wrap all of the toes in newspaper, making them thicker at the ends. You can also add a ball of paper at the back for a "heel." Tape well.

15 Wrap newspaper securely around the neck and tape it tightly. Make it thicker at the base and tapered toward the end.

16 To make the head, crumple a ball of paper and tape it tightly. This can be any shape you wish.

Using a utility knife, cut a hole in the back of the head.

17 Fit the head onto the neck. Tape it securely in place.

18 A bird needs a beak. Cut two cardboard triangles a little wider than the size and shape you want the finished beak to be.

To curve it a little, cut a V-shape in the center of the beak. Then tape it shut.

19 To make the beak three-dimensional, tape crumpled paper onto the cardboard. Tape the two halves together at the hinged end, as open or closed as you want them to be.

Set the beak aside. It will be attached later.

21 When her body is finished, glue Birdo in place on her eggs using carpenter's glue. Papier-mâché the eggs to the body. Then papier-mâché the legs.

Let her dry thoroughly, rotating her occasionally so that all sides can dry and mold won't form as a result of lack of air circulation.

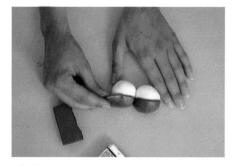

23 Make the eyes and the eyelids, if desired, from papier-mâché, commercial modelling clay, or from the papier-mâché pulp available at hobby stores.

20 Tear strips of newspaper and mix your flour-and-water paste. (See box.)

Papier-mâché the eggs and the beak. Apply paste over the area you wish to work on. Lay paper strips over the paste one at a time. Smooth down the strips with more paste.

Papier-mâché the whole bird except for her legs. Apply paste onto a good-sized section and papier-mâché as you go. Cover the bird with at least three layers of papier-mâché. You may have to work in several stages to do all of her.

Papier-mâché over the string. Any string that remains exposed can be cut later when Birdo is dry. Take your time.

22 Using a utility knife, cut a hole in Birdo's face and insert the beak. Tape it in place. Then papier-mâché the join thoroughly. Let Birdo dry again.

24 Apply a coat of gesso to the whole bird. Gesso is a white acrylic primer that will prevent the newsprint from showing through your paint.

25 With acrylic paint, paint your bird however you wish. The finish on Birdo was achieved by layering coats of semi-transparent paint. The acrylic paint was thinned a little with water, then sponged on with rags. Solid areas like the stomach, feet and beak were painted with a brush. (See FINISHING section for other treatments.)

27 Feathers are optional. Cut paper feathers from colored paper or use real ones. They can be glued in place with carpenter's glue or hot glue.

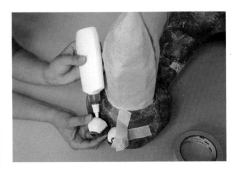

26 Attach the eyes with white carpenter's glue or hot glue. Tape them in place until they dry. If you don't want bulgy eyes on your bird, you can paint them on.

Monsters

W hether you enjoy watching old-time horror movies like "King Kong" or prefer the sophisticated contemporary films of the genre, it's a proven fact that people love monsters.

The lovable-hateable creatures in this section are rather human and not exactly terrifying, with pot bellies, googly eyes, fuzzy hair, snaggle teeth and a serious tendency to overeat. Even though they may be repulsive in some respects, they are kind of cuddly in another – and, for me, that's what monsters are all about.

If you create your own original monster, think of it as surreal. Adopt the human characteristics and habits that you see around you every day and exaggerate them for maximum impact. Beware of making your monster too human-looking. It can end up simply becoming a clown figure.

It is advisable to make a rough sketch of your monster-to-be. This will help you stay on track although it needn't be followed explicitly.

Improvise as you go, keeping in mind the properties of papier-mâché and how they relate to your creature. Hair, cloth and fur can be added at the finishing stage for extra effect, but the main part of your creature should be unhairy: warty, lumpy, wrinkly, whatever.

Whether you make the monsters featured here or create your own, the goal is fun for both the maker and the viewer.

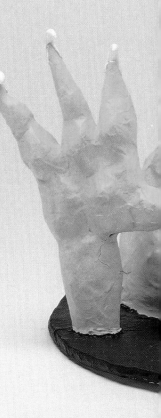

Sea Serpent

For hundreds of years, Sea Serpents have fascinated people the world over. They have reared their ugly heads in children's literature throughout the ages and have undulated through Oriental art and ancient carvings. The famous Loch Ness Monster is a well-loved fixture of Scottish lore.

This desk-top Sea Serpent is more lovable than scary and it's a good visual pun. It can swim straight or around corners and it can be made as long as you wish by adding or removing some humps.

This is a fairly quick project by papier-mâché standards. However, it does involve several drying times. A bright paint job is all your Sea Serpent really needs. You can add a snaky tongue, whiskers, points along its back or any other serpent-like details you can think of.

How to do it

MATERIALS:
Newspaper

Masking tape

Cup or jar approx. 3 inches (8 cm)
  in diameter, preferably tapered

Flour and water

Bread knife or similar knife
  with a long blade

Primer (gesso)

Acrylic paints and brushes

OPTIONAL:
Construction paper or bristol board

Utility knife or scissors

Carpenter's glue for paste or additions

Varnish

FINISHED SIZE:
Diameter: 6 inches (15 cm)
         (humps)

Height: 3½ inches (9 cm)
        (humps)

Height: 4 inches (10 cm)
        (head and tail)

1 To make the humps, create a cylinder at least 12 inches (30.5 cm) long by twisting a full sheet of newspaper. Add more newspaper as you need it. Make the cylinder as chubby as you'd like your serpent to be. Tape around the cylinder to hold it together.

2 Place the cylinder tightly around a cup or jar to form a donut shape.

3 Remove the donut-shaped cylinder and tape the overlapping ends together. Trim any excess at the ends for a uniform shape.

4 Create a cone for the tail from several layers of newspaper. The thickness of the fat end of the cone should more or less match the thickness of the donut.

Cut the tail to a length you feel is appropriate.

5 To make the cone bend, flatten it and cut V-shaped slashes in both sides. Bend the cone slightly and wrap it with masking tape. Stuff it with crumpled paper.

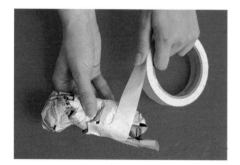

6 To make the head, form a short cylinder by twisting newspaper. Wrap it in tape.

Create the face by taping some crumpled paper to one side of the head. Be careful not to add too much or the head will tip over when it's finished.

8 Place the donut shape back on the cup or jar to keep it round while it dries.

7 Tear strips of newspaper and mix your flour-and-water paste. (See box.)

Papier-mâché your serpent, one piece at a time. Cover each piece in paste. One by one, lay strips of newspaper over the wet object and smooth them down with more paste. Don't worry about the uneven ends at the bottoms of the head and tail. They will be cut off later.

9 When the pieces are dry, you can cut them. Using a knife with a long blade, such as a bread knife, cut the donut into two unequal pieces to make two humps. One piece should comprise approximately two-thirds of the circle and the other one-third.

Papier-mâché Basics

NEWSPAPER STRIPS
- Newspaper has a grain. Tear it in the right direction and it will tear straight and evenly.

CLEANUP
- Place a plastic bag in your paste pot for quick cleanup.
- Coat your hands with Vaseline for easier paste removal.

PASTE RECIPE
- Add 1½ cups (350 mL) water to 1 cup (250 mL) flour. Mix it with your hands.
- Add 2 large spoonfuls of salt. Salt will help prevent mold from forming in your paste or on your project.
- Add about ¼ cup (50 mL) of carpenter's glue for extra strength (optional).

APPLICATION
- When spreading paste, apply it liberally.
- Do not dip the paper strips in the paste. Lay each strip on the wet paste area and smooth over with more paste.
- Apply at least three layers. Five is preferable.

DRYING
- Papier-mâché can take more than one day to dry.
- Test your project by touch. If it feels cool, it needs more time to dry.

10 Trim the head and tail so they stand up and are as high as you like. Papier-mâché over the cut bottoms and let them dry. If the face is too big, the head piece will fall over. Don't despair. Trim some of the face and papier-mâché over it. Let it dry.

11 Prime the sea serpent with gesso, a white acrylic primer that will prevent the newsprint from showing through your paint.

12 Add snaky details to your serpent if you wish. Cut points from colored paper and glue them to its back with carpenter's glue, mold a tongue or horns from modelling clay, or attach fur or feathers in a random pattern. (See FINISHING section for ideas.)

13 Paint the beast with acrylic paints. (See FINISHING section for ideas.)
   A final coat of varnish can help make your serpent more durable.

14 Place your Sea Serpent on your desk to guard important documents.

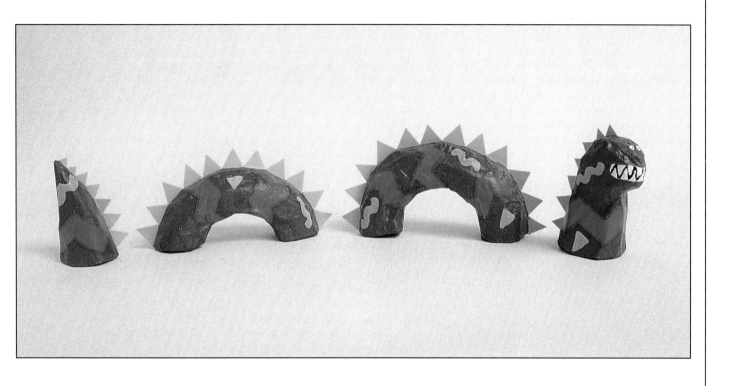

Suction Cup

Forget those cuddly, wimpy, furry toys that everyone loves to stick on their car windows. Here come some traffic-stopping, attention-getting monsters! These monsters don't need to be kept in the car. They are terrific on mirrors and windows at home, because they are great-looking from all angles.

Your monster doesn't have to resemble the ones shown here. Use your imagination when you create it. It can be longer, fatter or skinnier. It can have more legs and horns or googly eyes. You can also alter it at the painting and finishing stages with tufts of fur or feathers glued onto a bright paint job.

When making your monster, avoid the temptation to make it very large or the suction cups won't be strong enough to hold it up. Also remember that the legs have to be longer than any other part of the creature's body so that it will stick to the glass. So don't give it such a fat stomach that the legs don't reach beyond it.

This is not a very difficult project. The inner skeleton is made from coat hanger wire. You'll need to make a trip to the hardware store to buy the suction cups. Get the ones that are made for hanging a prism or stained glass on a window. These have a wire hook attached to the top. Buy medium or large ones at least 1½ inches (4 cm) in diameter. Smaller ones may not be strong enough to support your monster.

Monster

How to do it

MATERIALS:

3 wire coat hangers

2 pairs of pliers

Suction cups, at least 1½ inches
   (4 cm) in diameter

Newspaper

Masking tape

Medium-weight cardboard

Flour and water

Primer (gesso)

Acrylic paints and brushes

OPTIONAL:

Carpenter's glue for paste

Modelling clay or commercial
   papier-mâché pulp

FINISHED SIZE:

Length: 8 inches (20 cm)
           (excluding horns and tail)

Width: 10 inches (25.5 cm)
         (including legs)

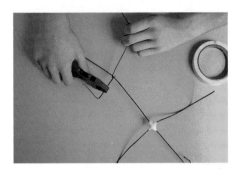

1 Untwist and straighten out three wire coat hangers. Place one in position to run through the middle of the body, from the end of the tail to the top of the head. Center the other two coat hangers across the first one at right angles. Either using pliers or by hand, twist the two hangers around the first hanger to form legs. Tape the hangers in place.

Cut the ends of all the hangers to the desired lengths, using pliers or wire cutters.

2 Remove the wire hook-rings from the suction cups. Using two pairs of pliers, bend the hook parts of the wires so that they are at right angles to the rings. Replace the rings onto the suction cups and tighten them if necessary.

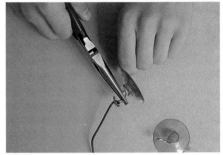

3 Curl the ends of the four legs to form closed loops.

Place the hooks of the suction cups through the loops in the ends of the legs. Tighten the hooks of the suction cups so they won't slip out of the loops.

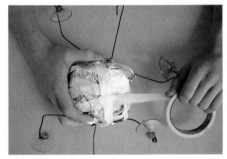

4 Form the body by crumpling newspaper around the midsection of the skeleton. Add paper until it is the size and shape you'd like it to be. Wrap the body tightly in tape.

Bend the legs into position. Stand your creature up and test to see that all of the suction cups are level and extend at least one inch beyond the belly.

5 Twist or crumple lengths of newspaper and wrap them around the legs. Keep wrapping until the legs are as chubby as you'd like. Wrap the legs in tape.

6 Create the head by crumpling newspaper and wrapping it around the end of the wire to form a ball. Tape around the ball and onto the body to keep the head in position.

7 Cut the feet shapes from medium-weight cardboard. The toes can be round or long and pointed.

On each cardboard foot, cut a slit into the foot beginning at the heel. Slide the slit onto the exposed hook above the suction cups. Tape the slit closed.

8 Tear your newspaper strips and mix your flour-and-water paste. (See box.)

Apply paste over the part of your monster that you want to start working on. One by one, lay strips of paper over the paste-covered section and smooth them down with more paste. Continue overlapping paper strips and pasting over them until you have at least three layers of papier-mâché. Progress over the entire creature until it is completely covered.

Papier-mâché Basics

NEWSPAPER STRIPS
- Newspaper has a grain. Tear it in the right direction and it will tear straight and evenly.

CLEANUP
- Place a plastic bag in your paste pot for quick cleanup.
- Coat your hands with Vaseline for easier paste removal.

PASTE RECIPE
- Add 1½ cups (350 mL) water to 1 cup (250 mL) flour. Mix it with your hands.
- Add 2 large spoonfuls of salt. Salt will help prevent mold from forming in your paste or on your project.
- Add about ¼ cup (50 mL) of carpenter's glue for extra strength (optional).

APPLICATION
- When spreading paste, apply it liberally.
- Do not dip the paper strips in the paste. Lay each strip on the wet paste area and smooth over with more paste.
- Apply at least three layers. Five is preferable.

DRYING
- Papier-mâché can take more than one day to dry.
- Test your project by touch. If it feels cool, it needs more time to dry.

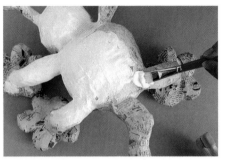

9 To make the feet three-dimensional, crumple small pieces of paper. Dip them in the paste and lay them on the toes. Papier-mâché around each toe with narrow strips of paper.

11 Prime your monster with gesso, a white acrylic primer that will prevent the newsprint from showing through your paint.

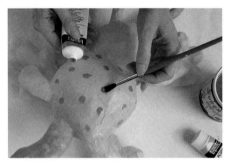

10 Bend the wire for the tail, making it as wavy or as curly as you wish. Wrap it in newspaper and tape it securely. Papier-mâché the tail.

This is also the time to make any bumps or lumps you want by crumpling and forming paper and taping it in place. Papier-mâché over these bumps or lumps.

Horns, teeth, toenails and the like can be made from commercial or homemade modelling clay (see FINISHING section page 142) or from the papier-mâché pulp available at hobby stores.

12 Using acrylic paints, paint your monster. Go as wild and bright as you like.

13 Stick your monster on the side window of your car and liven up rush hour.

Manhole Monster

Projects that are based on a visual illusion, like this Manhole Monster or the Sea Serpent, are satisfying because of their built-in joke. They also appear bigger and more impressive than they really are.

You can make any kind of creature coming out of a hole – chubby, warty, gangly, whatever you like. The one shown here is comical and happy, but yours can be mean and nasty. If you'd prefer a monster to hang on the wall, substitute a window for the hole and make the monster appear to be leaning through the window. If you intend this project for a coffee table or a desk, think about scale. Don't make it overly large.

Monsters present both challenges and simple solutions. They're meant to be unreal but there should be something vaguely familiar about them. It's no secret that the favorite animal at the zoo is the gorilla. It's unclear whether people love monkeys because they are reminded of themselves... or Uncle Harry. When you build your creatures, try to maintain simplicity in the construction. Because these are fantasy beasts, their forms can be very basic and proportions aren't that important. For best results, stick to solid, geometric shapes for the internal structures and embellish them.

This good-natured Manhole Monster is built from fairly simple geometric shapes. There are two or three stages of papier-mâché and the accompanying drying times. The hands and their placement are optional, as is the mood of the monster. For example, a monster climbing from a sewer could also be extremely crabby and covered with green slime. The choice is yours.

How to do it

MATERIALS:

Corrugated cardboard

Ruler

Utility knife or large scissors

Rubber cement or contact cement

Newspaper

Masking tape

Flour and water

Carpenter's glue or hot glue gun

Primer (gesso)

Paints and brushes

OPTIONAL:

Compass or 2 pencils and string

Foam board

Wire coat hanger

Carpenter's glue for paste

Toothpicks or pieces of cardboard

Modelling clay or commercial
   papier-mâché pulp

Finishing items

Varnish

FINISHED SIZE:

Diameter: 16 inches (40.5 cm)
   (of manhole)

Height: 15 inches (38 cm)

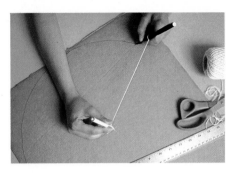

1 To make the manhole, measure and mark a circle on corrugated cardboard with a compass. If you don't have a compass large enough, make one by holding one pencil at the center of the circle. Tie string from this pencil to another pencil.

Cut out the circle with a utility knife or large scissors.

Using this circle as a pattern, make a second circle.

2 Glue the two circles together using two-coat rubber cement or contact cement. Read the label on the jar for instructions.

3 Make three balls of crumpled newspaper, one for the monster's chest and two for the shoulders. Tightly wrap all balls in tape, so that they are solid.

Position them on the cardboard circle and tape them in place.

4 To make the monster's long neck, roll several layers of newspaper to form a cone and tape it closed. Trim the bottom to make the cone the desired length. Adjust the diameter of the bottom of the cone so that it fits over the center ball which you have already made.

Stuff the cone with crumpled newspaper.

5 Position the cone over the center ball and tape it securely in place.

6 Form the monster's mouth by crumpling paper into two rounded beak-like shapes. The top half can be longer, shorter or wider than the bottom one, depending on the expression you want your monster to have.

7 Tape the jaws together at the hinged end, so that they are either open or closed. Set the jaws aside.

8 Draw the hand-shapes onto cardboard or foam board and cut them out. Position and tape them securely in place.

9 To secure the waving hand, cut a slot in the manhole and insert the wrist. It's a good idea to reinforce this hand with a piece of bent coat hanger wire that has been pushed through from below. Tape the wire both to the hand and underneath the base of the manhole.

10 Tear your newspaper strips and mix your flour-and-water paste. (See box.)

Apply paste all over the mouth. One by one, lay strips of paper onto the paste-covered section and smooth them down with more paste. Cover the mouth with three layers of papier-mâché. Set it aside to dry. You may need to prop it open with toothpicks or pieces of cardboard.

11 Using the same procedure, papier-mâché the monster. Cover the whole creature, including the manhole, with papier-mâché.

To create three-dimensional hands, add pieces of crumpled paper and tape them in place. Papier-mâché the hands. Allow everything to dry thoroughly.

Papier-mâché Basics

NEWSPAPER STRIPS
- Newspaper has a grain. Tear it in the right direction and it will tear straight and evenly.

CLEANUP
- Place a plastic bag in your paste pot for quick cleanup.
- Coat your hands with Vaseline for easier paste removal.

PASTE RECIPE
- Add 1½ cups (350 mL) water to 1 cup (250 mL) flour. Mix it with your hands.
- Add 2 large spoonfuls of salt. Salt will help prevent mold from forming in your paste or on your project.
- Add about ¼ cup (50 mL) of carpenter's glue for extra strength (optional).

APPLICATION
- When spreading paste, apply it liberally.
- Do not dip the paper strips in the paste. Lay each strip on the wet paste area and smooth over with more paste.
- Apply at least three layers. Five is preferable.

DRYING
- Papier-mâché can take more than one day to dry.
- Test your project by touch. If it feels cool, it needs more time to dry.

12 To attach the mouth, cut a hole in the front of the monster's head with a utilty knife.

13 Insert the mouth. Tape it in place. Papier-mâché over the mouth and onto the monster's head.
Add cheeks or other shapes to the head by adding crumpled paper. Papier-mâché over them with several layers.

14 Form nails, teeth, eyes and tongue. You can use papier-mâché, commercial or homemade modelling clay (see FINISHING section, page 142) or the papier-mâché pulp available at hobby stores.

15 Once the monster is completely dry, prime it with gesso, a white acrylic primer that will prevent newsprint from showing through your paint.

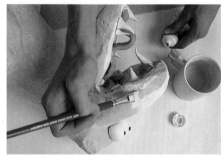

16 Using acrylic paint, paint your monster according to taste. Feathers and fluffy bits can also be glued on. (See FINISHING section for ideas.)
A coat of gloss varnish on the eyes and mouth can give them a wet look.

Pigasus

This is a very big pig. The bubblegum-pink color and hefty size of this porker make it impossible to miss. Big projects like this are impressive. They stop people in their tracks. Imperfect execution, uncomplicated designs, unsophisticated subject matter are all unimportant. Size is what matters most.

This project requires a large, elaborate inner structure. Piggy is extra fat and the wings are very small to accentuate the incongruity of this pink lump ever getting off the ground. The very small, black, beady eyes and the large ears also enhance its largeness. Most pigs designed for piggy banks and various sculptures are very smooth and rounded, as is Porky, the cartoon pig. I like the roughness of this pig. The lumpy properties of papier-mâché lend themselves perfectly to the cellulite-esque dimensions I wanted.

The pig's interior structure is made from foam board and chicken wire. Foam board is ideal for this project because it is very light. Also known as feather board, it is available at most hobby and art stores. If foam board is not available, corrugated cardboard can be substituted.

The foam board is cut and assembled to form a general, three-dimensional, internal shape. This is

then wrapped with chicken wire to give it a spherical frame.

The structural work in this project is more involved than the crumpled paper structures of other projects, and of course you need a fair amount of space to work in. The application of the papier-mâché must be done in stages, with the pig supported on boxes and rotated. Don't attempt to papier-mâché while the pig is suspended, or you'll end up lying on your back with paste dripping on your face, probably not unlike changing the oil under a Volkswagen Beetle.

Pigasus is a real showstopper at this enormous size, but you can also make smaller versions to hang in clusters or along a hallway. If you opt for a smaller variety, form the body from newspaper rather than chicken wire and tie nylon fishing line around the body for hanging.

Before you start this porcine project, check the size of your doors to be certain you don't end up like the man who built the ship in his basement and was reduced to praying for the sewers to back up so he could go sailing. If you don't have a large studio to work in, a garage or a sheltered outdoor location is fine.

How to do it

MATERIALS:
Newspaper
Masking tape
Flour and water
Foam board
Utility knife
Ruler
Wire cutters
Chicken wire
Gloves
Heavy gauge picture-hanging wire
Medium-weight cardboard
Wire coat hanger
Primer (gesso)
Acrylic paints and brushes

OPTIONAL:
Quilt batting
Carpenter's glue for paste
Modelling clay or commercial
   papier-mâché pulp
Small sticks or toothpicks
Finishing items
Glossy acrylic varnish
Hot glue

FINISHED SIZE:
Length: 40 inches (102 cm)
Width: 23 inches (58.5 cm)

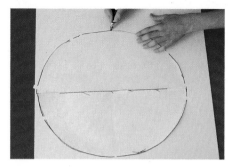

1 To create the inner body structure, begin by making three nearly-circular ovals which will be vertical inside the body. Cut the ovals from foam board or corrugated cardboard. The center one should be larger than the other two.

To make the shapes symmetrical and even, make a pattern from paper that you've folded in half. Lay your pattern on the board and trace around it. With a utility knife, cut the board along the line.

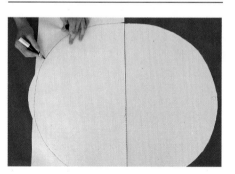

2 Using a pattern as above, cut out a fourth oval, nearly twice as large as the others. To determine the size of the large oval, make its center-crosswise diameter match the lengthwise diameter of the largest of the three ovals. The front of this fourth oval should be slightly pointed, not as rounded as the rear end.

This oval will be horizontal inside the body, at right angles to the others.

3 Intersect the four ovals to assemble the body structure. Use a ruler to measure and cut slots halfway across the centers of the three smaller ovals and three slots at equal distances on the largest oval, as shown.

4 Slide the slots of the small ovals into the slots of the large oval. If necessary, add pieces of cardboard between the ovals and tape them in position to maintain rigidity.

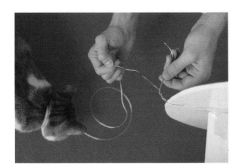

5 Determine which side will be the top of the pig. Make holes approximately two inches from the top edges of the ovals. Thread picture-hanging wire through the holes and secure it by twisting the wire tightly. This will be used to hang the finished pig.

6 Cut a length of chicken wire to fit around the pig's structure. Use wire cutters. Gloves are recommended for handling the chicken wire.

7 Wrap the chicken wire around the pig's body with the ends of the mesh overlapping. Secure it by bending the overlapping points down and around the underlying chicken wire.

Draw the picture-hanging wire through and wrap it around the chicken wire several times for strength when the pig is hung up.

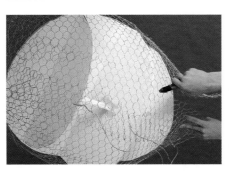

8 To make the mesh conform to the pig's body shape, cut into the chicken wire from the ends and overlap the edges. Secure the overlaps by bending the points under to catch the underlying mesh.

9 OPTIONAL: To prevent the texture of chicken wire from showing through the papier-mâché, cover the body structure with a thin layer of quilt batting. Then wrap the body with masking tape. Several layers of newspaper can be substituted for the quilt batting.

10 To make the pig's head, crumple newspaper and continue wrapping it in layers until you have a "pig-headed" sized ball. Wrap it securely in tape. The ball should be dense and solid.

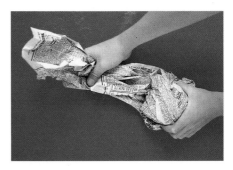

11 Form the nose by rolling up strips of newspaper. Wrap it in tape.

Papier-mâché Basics

NEWSPAPER STRIPS

- **Newspaper has a grain. Tear it in the right direction and it will tear straight and evenly.**

CLEANUP

- **Place a plastic bag in your paste pot for quick cleanup.**
- **Coat your hands with Vaseline for easier paste removal.**

PASTE RECIPE

- **Add 1½ cups (350 mL) water to 1 cup (250 mL) flour. Mix it with your hands.**
- **Add 2 large spoonfuls of salt. Salt will help prevent mold from forming in your paste or on your project.**
- **Add about ¼ cup (50 mL) of carpenter's glue for extra strength (optional).**

APPLICATION

- **When spreading paste, apply it liberally.**
- **Do not dip the paper strips in the paste. Lay each strip on the wet paste area and smooth over with more paste.**
- **Apply at least three layers. Five is preferable.**

DRYING

- **Papier-mâché can take more than one day to dry.**
- **Test your project by touch. If it feels cool, it needs more time to dry.**

12 Tape the nose to the front of the head.

Cut triangle-shaped ears from medium-weight cardboard. Make a V-shaped cut in the base of each ear. Pull the sections together to close the gap and tape it shut. This will give the ears some dimension.

Position the ears and tape them securely on the head.

13 Tear strips of newspaper and mix your flour-and-water paste. (See box.)

Cover the entire head, including the ears, with paste. One by one, lay paper strips on the paste-covered area and smooth them down with more paste. Continue applying paper strips and building layers. Progress until the entire head has been covered with at least five layers of papier-mâché.

Allow the head to dry. You can thicken the ears by adding crumpled paper to them and applying papier-mâché. You may need to prop up the ears with small sticks or toothpicks while they dry.

14 Form the front and hind legs by crumpling paper into four pork chop shapes for the upper legs. Make the pork chops for the hind legs larger than the front ones.

Make four lower leg shapes from crumpled and twisted paper. Keep them bent slightly for a piggy shape and tape them securely. Wrap both upper and lower legs in tape.

15 Tape the upper legs to the corresponding lower leg sections.

16 Using a utility knife, prepare the head for attachment to the body by trimming the back of the head so that it will conform to the body shape.

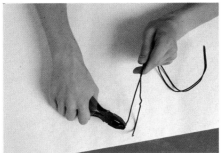

18 Untwist a wire coat hanger and straighten it. Bend it double, then twist it to form a pleasing pig tail shape. Bend the two ends back to form a hook.

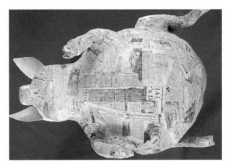

20 Papier-mâché the whole pig in stages, pasting and applying the papier-mâché on one section at a time. You will probably have to take the pig down, turn it over and support it on a cardboard box to do the underside. Cover the pig completely with at least five layers of papier-mâché. Let it dry thoroughly.

The wings are attached after priming the pig to prevent them from being in the way.

17 Hang up your pig. Using strong, wide masking tape, secure the legs and head where you want them to go.

With crumpled newspaper, fill in around the head to form a neck, Systematically cover the entire pig with newspaper, filling in and padding any areas that require it.

Tape around and around the entire pig to keep it solid.

Form cup-shaped, cleft hooves onto the ends of the legs by crumpling newspaper and taping it in position.

19 Insert the hook into the body and catch it in the underlying chicken wire.

Wrap the tail with crumpled lengths of newspaper to achieve the required thickness. Tape securely around the tail and onto the body.

21 Prime the pig with gesso, a white acrylic primer that will prevent newsprint from showing through your paint.

22 Cut wing shapes from foam board or cardboard. Tape them in position and papier-mâché them to the body. Add crumpled paper dipped in paste and papier-mâché for a three-dimensional form, if you wish. If the wings threaten to fall down from the weight of the papier-mâché, loop and tie string around them to hold them up. When the papier-mâché is dry, cut away any excess, exposed string.

Prime the wings with gesso.

24 Form the eyes from papier-mâché, a commercial or homemade modelling clay (see FINISHING section, page 142) or the papier-mâché pulp available at hobby stores.

25 Glossy acrylic varnish on the eyes and hooves adds sparkle. To finish the wings you can either paint on feathers or apply real or paper ones with hot glue.

23 Paint your pig the perfect piggy-pink. If you mix the shade, prepare a good amount to start. You'll need enough for two coats. Paint the hooves and nostrils black. (See FINISHING section for other treatments.)

26 Clear the runway and notify the tower – Pigasus is ready for takeoff.

Refrigerator Raider

H ere is the answer to that age-old question: "Who ate the ice cream, the last of the milk, and the leftover broccoli?" Here is the one that rummages in the night, leaving dirty dishes on the kitchen counter, bits of egg yolk drying on the floor and crumbs and guck in the sink. Your own fridge-a-raider will put an end to domestic arguments.

Refrigerator Raider is the most ambitious of the Monster projects. He is smaller than Pigasus, but far more involved. He requires more work space than a small table and a lot of detail work for the props.

R.R.'s body structure is made from wire coat hangers and formed, crumpled newspapers wrapped in masking tape. It can also be made from chicken wire, if you prefer. The "Smoking is Monstrous" monster is a variation on the same body structure. The legs, tail and basic wire skeleton is the same, but the top portion is built of chicken wire. (See pages

15 and 17, for more information on chicken wire construction.)

Use your imagination when it comes to food for R.R. You don't have to make the same snacks as those I have prepared. I'm sure he would enjoy melted ice cream, a bunch of grapes, some leftover cauliflower or salad equally well. Use real food packages and containers and just add some papier-mâché food either inside or spilling from the containers. Don't use real food. Even something as dry as crackers will deteriorate over time.

Refrigerator Raider is an advanced and ambitious project. Before you tackle this monster, you should be well acquainted with papier-mâché and its properties. The instructions are fairly general for the food portion of this project to inspire you to create rather than duplicate.

Placed in the kitchen or dining room, Refrigerator Raider will provide lots of entertainment, as well as encouragement to stick to that diet.

How to do it

MATERIALS:

10 wire coat hangers
Pliers
Wide masking tape
Aluminum foil
Newspaper
Foam board or corrugated cardboard
Utility knife
Marker
Flour and water
Primer (gesso)
Acrylic paints and brushes
Hot glue gun or carpenter's glue

OPTIONAL:

String
Carpenter's glue for paste
Food containers
Modelling clay or commercial
    papier-mâché pulp
Plywood
Jigsaw or band saw

FINISHED SIZE:

Height: 23 inches (58.5 cm)
Width: 17 inches (43 cm)
        (including thighs)

1 Create a fat body for the monster by stretching two wire coat hangers into hoop shapes. Don't untwist them or straighten the hooks.

Lay one hoop on top of the other, with the hooks on opposite sides. Tape the hoops together.

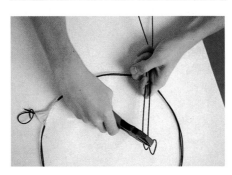

2 Using pliers, bend the hooks into tight loops. These will act as hip joints.

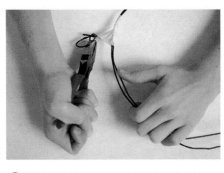

3 To make leg skeletons, untwist and straighten two coat hangers. Bend each in half.

Bend the curved end of the leg-hangers over to form a hook.

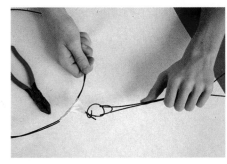

4 Slip the hooks into the hip joints. Squeeze the hooks tightly, so that the legs won't slide out but will still be movable. Both legs should point forward.

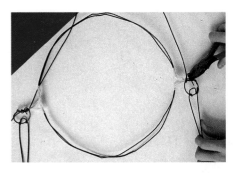

5 To create the tail structure, untwist and straighten two coat hangers. Twist the end of each wire onto the hip joints. The legs should point one way and the tail-wires the opposite way.

Tape the tail-wires to the sides of the hoops. They will form a long point. Tape the loose ends together.

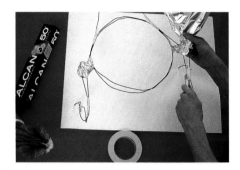

6 Bend the legs to form knees. Wrap tape around each thigh and calf, to prevent the wires from spreading apart.

Tape the hip joints securely and wrap them in aluminum foil, crushing it tightly, to help create stability. The body is now supported by the legs and the end of the tail.

7 Create two-toed feet by bending two more coat hangers as shown. (The hooks of the hangers will be heels.) You may add extra toes, if you wish, by twisting pieces of wire of the appropriate length onto the hangers.

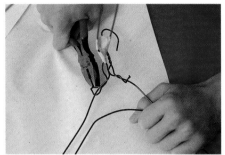

8 Attach the feet by twisting the leg-wires onto the feet on either side of the heel.

9 To help prevent the knees and ankles from collapsing, pack the hollow side of each with crumpled newspaper and tape around it.

If your structure is wobbly, you can tie string from the legs to the tail and body. The string can be added at any stage and can be left in place until the monster has been completed.

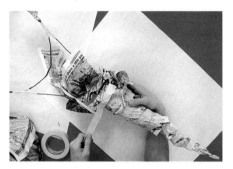

10 Start forming the tail by stuffing crumpled newspaper between the two wires. Wrap it loosely in tape. The tail can be left straight, cut short or curled.

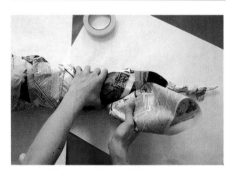

11 Wrap crumpled newspaper around the tail, covering the paper and the wires. Continue adding and taping more newspaper, until the shape of the tail is pleasing. Tightly wrap the tail in masking tape. The tail should be quite solid.

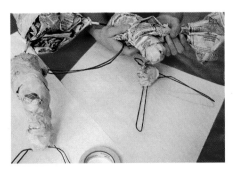

12 Wrap the legs tightly in strips of twisted or crumpled newspaper. Start with the thighs and work your way down the legs, tapering to the ankles. Build up more newspaper for shape on the thigh and calf, if desired. Wrap the legs tightly in tape.

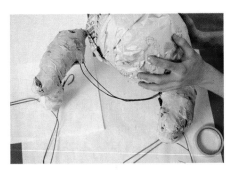

13 Form a fat, dense body-ball. To do this, crumple paper and roll it in layers, until the ball is slightly larger than the diameter of the hoops. Wrap the ball tightly in tape.

Place the ball onto the hoops. It will sit high.

14 Add paper to the outside of the ball, covering the wires. Be sure to pad the areas where the legs and body join, for a smooth connection. Tape everything well.

Form the toes and the heels by wrapping the wire with crumpled strips of newspaper, tapering to the ends of the toes. Tape the feet well.

15 To begin shaping the upper body and the mouth, cut half of an oblong shape from foam board or corrugated cardboard. The width at the flat end should match the diameter of the body-ball.

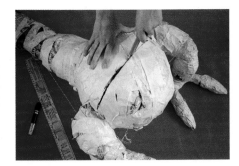

16 Draw a straight line from side to side across the middle of the monster's body. Using a utility knife, cut along your line.

17 Fit the flat end of the foam board into the cut. It should be flush at the sides and sit straight. Adjust your cut, if necessary. Tape the foam board in position.

18 Create a bottom jaw by crumpling and forming newspaper into a flat, half-circle shape. Tape it in place at the base of the foam board. Using crumpled paper, fill in around the jaw and create a bottom lip. Tape the lip in place.

19 Twist and crumple newspaper and begin building shape along the top and sides of the mouth. Create whatever shape you feel is appropriate. Your monster can have an overbite, smiling lips or any facial expression you like.

20 Form rolls of fat from crumpled and rolled newspaper. Stack and tape them tightly up the monster's back.

21 To create four arms, untwist and straighten two wire coat hangers. Cut them in half, using pliers or wire cutters. Push the cut end of each hanger into the side of the foam board, about one-half to two-thirds of the way in. Tape down any stray ends that poked through the foam board during insertion.

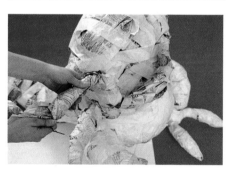

22 Bend the arms to the position you'd like them to remain in. Wrap them in newspaper to give them shape. Wrap them well with tape. Leave wire protruding from the ends of the arms.

Don't worry about the hands. They will be made later.

Papier-mâché Basics

NEWSPAPER STRIPS
- **Newspaper has a grain. Tear it in the right direction and it will tear straight and evenly.**

CLEANUP
- **Place a plastic bag in your paste pot for quick cleanup.**
- **Coat your hands with Vaseline for easier paste removal.**

PASTE RECIPE
- **Add 1¹/₂ cups (350 mL) water to 1 cup (250 mL) flour. Mix it with your hands.**
- **Add 2 large spoonfuls of salt. Salt will help prevent mold from forming in your paste or on your project.**
- **Add about ¹/₄ cup (50 mL) of carpenter's glue for extra strength (optional).**

APPLICATION
- **When spreading paste, apply it liberally.**
- **Do not dip the paper strips in the paste. Lay each strip on the wet paste area and smooth over with more paste.**
- **Apply at least three layers. Five is preferable.**

DRYING
- **Papier-mâché can take more than one day to dry.**
- **Test your project by touch. If it feels cool, it needs more time to dry.**

23 Tear your newspaper strips and mix your flour-and-water paste. (See box.)

Apply paste over an area of your monster. One by one, lay paper strips over the paste-covered area and smooth them down with more paste. Continue adding overlapping paper strips until you have applied at least three layers of papier-mâché. Progress over the entire monster, except the hands.

Either apply the papier-mâché in stages, allowing each area to dry, or apply it all over the monster. If you do the entire monster in one sitting, rotate it while it is drying. This will prevent mold from forming due to a lack of air circulation.

25 Decide which props you would like your monster to hold in its hands. You can use clean food containers or you can create papier-mâché food.

Form crumpled newspaper into the appropriate food shapes. Tape them well and papier-mâché them. Simple shapes are best, with paint adding realism.

The monster's long, pointy tongue can also be shaped from papier-mâché at this stage.

27 Remove the props and add form to the fingers by wrapping them with newspaper. Build up paper at the base of the fingers to create a pad and to give the fingers more stability. Test to be certain that the props still fit into the hands. Now papier-mâché the hands.

28 Prime your monster and its props with gesso, a white acrylic primer that will prevent the newsprint from showing through your paint.

24 To make fingers, cut eight pieces of eight-inch (20 cm) coat hanger wire.

Using pliers, twist two of these onto each hand, one on each side of the existing wire. Each hand now has three fingers.

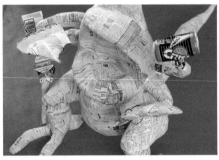

26 Position the props in the monster's hands, bending the wires into place to hold each prop. Cut any wires that are too long, using pliers or wire cutters. All props will ultimately be glued onto the finished hands. Any that are loose should be stabilized at that stage.

29 Using acrylic paints, paint your monster however you like: lizard-like, bright and cheerful, scaly, or clownish. (See FINISHING section for ideas.)

30 Paint your props in appropriate colors.

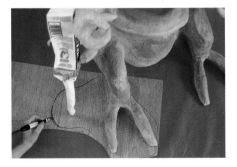

31 OPTIONAL: If you wish to make a puddle for melted ice cream, or spilt milk, soda or juice, draw an outline onto ¼-inch (0.5 cm) plywood. Cut out the shape with a jigsaw or band saw. Prime it with gesso and paint it the appropriate color. Glue it in place with a hot glue gun.

32 Using commercial or homemade modelling clay (see FINISHING section, page 142) or the papier-mâché pulp available at hobby stores, form the monster's eyes, teeth and any toenails and fingernails you desire. Paint them appropriate colors.

Attach them with a hot glue gun or carpenter's glue. The teeth and nails will be stronger if they are glued into individual holes.

33 Place the props in the monster's hands and glue them in place with a hot glue gun.

Examine your monster to decide whether it is messy enough. If not, create more slopped food and glue it in place.

All the objects in this section can be used around the house: some for practical purposes, others as sculptures or ornaments. The Trays, Paperweights, Napkin Rings and Bowls are both useful and decorative, though none of these items are meant for heavy or utility use. The Mermaid and Jennifer, the life-sized girl, are both strictly decorative sculptures.

The useful projects in this section are some of the fastest, easiest and impressive ones in the book. The Bowl, for example, is a beautiful and sophisticated-looking piece of art that can be finished very differently each time it's made. To make these items practical, certain measures may be necessary for waterproofing and strengthening them.

These projects make great gifts and it can be self-motivating to work on several items at once. While one project is drying, another needs painting, or another group can be initiated. While the papier-

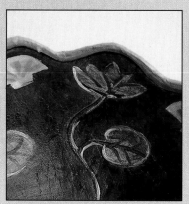   

Home

mâché stage can be therapeutic, the painting stage is exhilarating. Transforming the drab objects that you've created into beautiful, colorful pieces makes all the slogging worthwhile.

On the other hand, the Mermaid and Jennifer are two of the most involved and intricate projects in the book. These are ambitious projects. While a talented beginner might work on the mermaid (which is formed from paper and has some leeway as far as proportions and finishing skills), only those who have made other items and are thoroughly familiar with papier-mâché and its properties should attempt to create Jennifer or a similar sculpture.

I have kept the instructions for Jennifer general to enable you to create the sculpture of your choice without having to duplicate. A child eating ice cream, jumping hopscotch, or playing with a yo-yo are all good subjects. Including a dog or cat in your sculpture can turn it into a scene and add scale.

Decor

Bowls

Fast, simple, impressive and practical, these bowls have the quintessential, handcrafted papier-mâché look that makes them one-of-a-kind. They can be made in virtually any size. Everyone will want one of your original bowls. Don't forget to sign them.

Their individual paint jobs adapt these bowls to any room, as a piece of sculpture or as a useful repository for odds and ends. A water and sea design for the bathroom holds guest soaps or cosmetics. A large watermelon or vegetable pattern for the kitchen makes a striking fruit bowl. Smaller, fanciful bowls finished in découpage or textured designs are ideal for keeping watches and favorite pieces of jewellery in one place in the bedroom.

To make this bowl, you will mold papier-mâché over the outside of an existing bowl. When you select your mold-bowl, keep in mind the size and shape you want your finished bowl to be. A semi-circle shape is best, as it allows the papier-mâché to release easily and its shape is pleasing to the eye. A bowl with a spout is unsuitable, particularly since the new bowl should never be used for holding or pouring liquids, or as a mixing or utility bowl. Papier-mâché bowls are designed for light or decorative use only.

There are two ways to mold your bowl. The simpler method is to cover the mold-bowl with Vaseline and papier-mâché over it. A bowl made this way must be thoroughly dry in order to release from the mold. This means you cannot apply very many layers of papier-mâché or the bowl may rot or develop mildew before drying. Using this method, you will end up with a finished bowl that is fairly weak but beautifully smooth and symmetrical. When additional layers of papier-mâché are added after unmolding, the Vaseline-method bowls tend to become distorted and wrinkled.

The second way to mold your bowl is to cover the mold with newspaper followed by plastic food wrap, and then apply papier-mâché over it. Don't lay the plastic directly onto the mold-bowl as the papier-mâché won't release properly. This method allows you to apply up to twenty layers of papier-mâché. However, when you unmold your bowl, it won't be completely dry and its shape will change as it finishes drying. Personally, I like the odd and interesting shapes that these bowls assume. They look more handcrafted and less commercial than those made with the Vaseline method and they are far stronger.

The following instructions are for the newspaper-and-plastic-wrap release method. Instructions for the Vaseline-release method are listed as ALTERNATIVE.

Although this is a fairly fast project by papier-mâché standards, there are still drying times and finishing details involved. The impressive sizes of the bowls and the scope of interesting paint treatments make this an extremely rewarding project, and one that children can successfully accomplish with a little help.

How to do it

MATERIALS:

Plastic or glass bowl to use as a mold
Newspaper
Scissors
Masking tape
Plastic food wrap
Flour and water
Utility knife
Primer (gesso)
Acrylic paints and brushes

OPTIONAL:

Vaseline
Carpenter's glue for paste
Compass
Corrugated cardboard

FINISHED SIZE:

Diameter: 14 inches (35.5 cm)

1 The exterior of your bowl will act as a mold. Prepare it as follows. With scissors, cut a sheet of newspaper into a circle larger than is needed to cover the exterior of your bowl. You can do this by folding the newspaper into quarters and cutting the open sides into a quarter-circle.

2 Cut into the paper circle from the edge, as though slicing a pie, but don't go through the center. Slash the circle in this way eight times or more, with the slashes fairly evenly spaced.

3 With your bowl right side up, center the paper circle under it. Bring each slashed piece of paper up and over the edge of the bowl and tape it in place, adjusting the newspaper to the shape of the bowl until it is completely covered.

4 Tape over any cuts, tears or large creases so that the paper conforms to the shape of the bowl.

5 Place a sheet of plastic wrap over the newspaper and tape it to the inside of the bowl as you did with the newspaper. Overlap sheets of plastic wrap and smooth down the edges to make it cling, until the newspaper is completely covered. Tape it to the *inside* of the bowl only. There should be no gaps in the plastic and no tape on the outside of the bowl. The bowl will have a slightly spongy feeling.

7 Tear strips of newspaper and mix your flour-and-water paste. (See box.)

Apply paste all over your bowl. One by one, lay paper strips onto the paste-covered area and smooth them down with more paste. Overlap the paper strips as you go.

ALTERNATIVE: For the first layer of papier-mâché only, do not apply paste over your bowl. Instead, dip the strips into the paste before laying them on the bowl. Apply subsequent layers as usual. (See box.)

NEWSPAPER STRIPS
- Newspaper has a grain. Tear it in the right direction and it will tear straight and evenly.

CLEANUP
- Place a plastic bag in your paste pot for quick cleanup.
- Coat your hands with Vaseline for easier paste removal.

PASTE RECIPE
- Add 1½ cups (350 mL) water to 1 cup (250 mL) flour. Mix it with your hands.
- Add 2 large spoonfuls of salt. Salt will help prevent mold from forming in your paste or on your project.
- Add about ¼ cup (50 mL) of carpenter's glue for extra strength (optional).

APPLICATION
- When spreading paste, apply it liberally.
- Do not dip the paper strips in the paste. Lay each strip on the wet paste area and smooth over with more paste.
- Apply at least three layers. Five is preferable.

DRYING
- Papier-mâché can take more than one day to dry.
- Test your project by touch. If it feels cool, it needs more time to dry.

6 ALTERNATIVE: Place your bowl upside down and smear a thick layer of Vaseline all over the outside of it. Be certain that it is entirely covered and that there are no bare patches on the surface or near the edges.

8 Vary the pattern of the papier-mâché to avoid any weakness that can occur by having strips piled evenly on top of each other. Alternate between an accordian pattern, in which you work from side to side (shown in step 7) and a spiral pattern, in which you progress in a circular pattern (shown here). Continue until the entire bowl has approximately fifteen to twenty layers of papier-mâché. This can be done in one sitting.

ALTERNATIVE: Apply only five to eight layers of papier-mâché. Allow to dry thoroughly.

9 When the papier-mâché feels dry to the touch, trim the excess material around the edge with a utility knife while the mold-bowl is still inside it. Hold your knife in as vertical a position as possible.

ALTERNATIVE: Do not trim your bowl now. Trim your bowl later, when it is off the mold. The edge is needed to hold onto for unmolding.

10 To unmold the bowl, remove the tape from the inside and lift the original bowl out.

11 The newspaper and the plastic wrap can now be peeled off. The inside of the bowl will still be damp.

At this point the bowl will begin to assume its own unique shape. If you let it sit on its bottom and it is still fairly wet, it will become oval or oblong. For a more circular bowl, turn it upside down to dry. Placing it on a heat register can speed up the drying process. In any case, it will not be a perfect circle. This is what gives your bowl character. Allow it to dry thoroughly.

12 ALTERNATIVE: To remove the mold from the bowl, grasp the ragged edge of the papier-mâché in one hand and grip the inside bowl with the other. If the Vaseline was applied properly and the papier-mâché is *completely* dry, the two bowls will separate easily. If they won't come apart easily, allow more drying time.

13 ALTERNATIVE: To remove some of the Vaseline from the inside of your bowl, wash with a damp, soapy cloth. Wipe the bowl well. Most of the grease will be absorbed into the papier-mâché.

Trim the edge of the bowl. (See step 9.) Avoid leaning on your bowl while you cut because it could collapse.

14 Decide between keeping a straight edge or making it jagged or wavy. To trim the edge, draw your design on the inside. Then cut along it with a utility knife. You may need someone to hold the bowl steady for you while you cut.

15 Finish the edge by tearing a long strip of paper. Tear into the sides of the strip to make it conform to the bowl. Smooth some paste along the edge of the bowl, then lay the paper strip lengthwise along it and smooth it down with more paste. This procedure works well for both straight and uneven edges.

16 OPTIONAL: Many bowls look very interesting when they sit at an angle, but if you want your bowl to sit straight, give it a flat bottom. Use a compass or trace around the rim of a cup to draw a circle on the center of the bottom of your bowl. Cut out the circle with a utility knife.

Cut a circle from corrugated cardboard that is the same size or slightly smaller than the circle that you cut in the bowl.

17 OPTIONAL: With the bowl upright on a flat surface, tape the cardboard circle in place in the hole. Papier-mâché over the cardboard and the tape.

18 Prime your bowl with gesso, a white, acrylic primer that will prevent the newsprint from showing through your paint.

19 Using acrylic paints, paint your bowl according to your own design. (See FINISHING section for ideas.)

Paperweights

Papier-mâché is a very light material and it may seem odd to talk about papier-mâché paperweights, the equivalent of a feather doorstop. The trick to making these paperweights heavy is to build them around rocks. This is another example of the inexpensive nature of this craft. A trip to the beach or a field for some stones, a few newspapers and some flour and water are all readily available. Add some acrylic paints for

finishing and you have some nicely detailed, useful and attractive pieces.

These paperweights are quite small compared to many other projects in this book. The small size of these objects means more intricate work at the papier-mâché stage. The most tricky areas are the small indentations, hills and valleys, where strips of paper won't conform to the contours. To overcome this, tear your paper strips no more than ½ inch (1.25 cm) wide. As you apply the strips, tear into the sides. This will allow each strip to fan out on one side and overlap itself on the other side. You can also proceed by applying a rough layer of papier-mâché and letting it dry. Then tear off any ragged parts and

apply a smooth layer. Patience and perseverance will be rewarded.

Choose rocks that fit comfortably in the palm of your hand. Paperweights need to be readily movable and anything larger may be more suitable as a doorstop. Determine what each rock will become by assessing its shape. Think about where it will be used. If you find a long rock, it can be made into a fat pencil for the office, a hotdog for the kitchen (good for holding down napkins), or a fish for the bathroom. A spherical rock can be the body of a sleeping cat, bird or spider, and so on. Choose your finished objects with simple shapes in mind for best results.

The impact of these paperweights, as for most papier-mâché projects, lies in the finishing. A detailed or bold design transforms an ordinary object, as do decorative and molded clay pieces that can be added on.

It's worth making several paperweights at once. Everyone will want one and they make great gifts. Don't forget to sign them!

Part of the fun of this project is in collecting your stones. But please don't pilfer your stones or rocks from other people's gardens or public parks. Most beaches and open fields are good rock-hunting grounds. Remember that farms are private property too. Most farmers don't mind their stones being removed if you ask permission first.

How to do it

MATERIALS:
Rocks
Newspaper
Masking tape
Flour and water
Primer (gesso)
Acrylic paints and brushes

OPTIONAL:
Carpenter's glue for paste
String or nylon fishing line
Utility knife
Modelling clay or commercial
   papier-mâché pulp
Finishing items
Carpenter's glue or hot glue gun
Varnish

FINISHED SIZES:
Varied, depending on size of stones

1 Examine your rock and determine what its shape reminds you of. Because you are going to add to it, all that needs to be decided is a general shape for your paperweight. A flat stone, for example, can become a fried egg or a turtle.

2 To form your paperweight's basic shape, add newspaper where it's needed and tape it in place. Crumpled newspaper gives a rounded effect – perfect for a burger bun. Twisted paper that is wrapped in tape forms cylinders that can be fingers on a baseball glove or that can be wound around the rock to create the white of a fried egg. The more forming you do now, the less work you'll have during the papier-mâché stage. Tape the paper-shaping well. It should be dense and solid.

3 Tear your strips of newspaper and mix your flour-and-water paste. (See box.)

Cover your paperweight in paste. One by one, lay overlapping strips of paper onto the paste-covered area and smooth them down with more paste.

Use narrow strips on intricate areas and tear into the sides of the paper strips to help them conform to curves. Progress until there are at least three layers of papier-mâché covering the entire paperweight.

4 Paperweights that won't stay in position to dry can be tied in place with string or nylon fishing line. Papier-mâché over the string. When the papier-mâché is dry, the excess string can be cut away. Let everything dry thoroughly.

Examine your object. If there are any parts you wish to change, either cut them away with a utility knife or add more crumpled paper. Papier-mâché over the corrections.

5 Prime your paperweight with gesso, a white acrylic primer that will prevent newsprint from showing through your paint.

6 When the primer is dry, you can start adding details that are appropriate for your paperweight. Some items – teeth, eyes, mustard, horns and the like – can be formed from commercial or homemade modelling clay (see FINISHING section, page 142) or from the papier-mâché pulp available in hobby stores. Only add the details that you wish to paint along with your paperweight. Some items are best painted separately and added later. (See step 8.)

7 Paint your object using acrylic paints. (See FINISHING section for ideas.)

8 When your paint has dried thoroughly, various finishing and textural details can be added for heightened effect. Real sesame seeds lend credibility to the hamburger and hot dog buns. Plush material can provide a cuddly accent. Lace accentuates the underpants and Velcro self-adhesive dots become the spots on the caterpillar. Sequins, buttons, ribbon, dried leaves and flowers are other decorative options.

Attach accent bits and pieces with carpenter's glue or hot glue. (See FINISHING section.)

9 If you wish, a final, protective coat of acrylic varnish can be applied.

Papier-mâché Basics

NEWSPAPER STRIPS
- **Tear with the grain for straight strips.**

CLEANUP
- **Place a plastic bag in your paste pot for quick cleanup.**

PASTE RECIPE
- **Add 1½ cups (350 mL) water to 1 cup (250 mL) flour. Mix it with your hands.**
- **Add 2 large spoonfuls of salt. Salt will help prevent mold from forming.**
- **Add about ¼ cup (50 mL) of carpenter's glue for extra strength (optional).**

APPLICATION
- **Apply paste generously.**
- **Do not dip the paper strips in the paste. Lay each strip on the wet paste area and smooth over with more paste.**
- **Apply at least three layers. Five is preferable.**

DRYING
- **Papier-mâché can take more than one day to dry.**
- **Test your project by touch. If it feels cool, it needs more time to dry.**

Napkin Rings

Napkin rings are one of the small touches that add color, mood and style to a table setting. Featured in this project are two sets of eight napkin rings. They have a rough, handcrafted feeling which complements the texture of papier-mâché. These napkin rings can be bright and whimsical additions to a casual family dinner, picnic or a buffet.

It's worth making several sets of rings once you've started. You can vary the themes to keep things interesting. Try different cheeses, stylized cats and mice, breads, rolls and bagels, and of course, fruits and vegetables. A set of napkin rings with coordinating napkins or a bottle of wine makes a welcome and attractive gift.

Although it may be faster to make the fruits and vegetables from homemade or commercial modelling clay or from the papier-mâché pulp available at hobby stores, you can lose the handcrafted appearance and vivacious mood of these pieces if the fruits and vegetables are too smooth and manufactured-looking. They can also become too heavy, making the rings tip sideways.

Once they are painted and varnished, the rings will be water-resistant and can be cleaned with a damp cloth. They should not be submerged in water or put in the dishwasher.

How to do it

MATERIALS:

Corrugated cardboard
Ruler and utility knife
Masking tape
Newspaper
Flour and water
Primer (gesso)
Acrylic paints and brushes
Lightweight cardboard
Carpenter's glue or hot glue gun
Varnish

OPTIONAL:

Rolling pin
Tissue paper
Wallpaper paste
Modelling clay or commercial
  papier-mâché pulp
Emery board or sandpaper

FINISHED SIZE:

Outside circumference of ring:
  6½ inches (16.5 cm)

Papier-mâché Basics

NEWSPAPER STRIPS
• Newspaper has a grain. Tear it in the right direction and it will tear straight and evenly.

CLEANUP
• Place a plastic bag in your paste pot for quick cleanup.

PASTE RECIPE
• Add 1½ cups (350 mL) water to 1 cup (250 mL) flour and 2 large spoonfuls of salt. Mix it with your hands.

APPLICATION
• When spreading paste, apply it liberally.
• Do not dip the paper strips in the paste. Lay them on the wet paste area and smooth with more paste.
• Apply at least three layers. Five is preferable.

1 Using a utility knife and a ruler, measure, mark and cut strips of corrugated cardboard 1½ x 6 inches (4 x 15.25 cm). Double-thickness cardboard is preferable and can be found in boxes that carry heavy shipments like liquor or books. Ensure that the corrugations run crosswise inside the strips. When you look at a long edge, you should see a line of holes.

Working from one end of a strip to the other, crush the cardboard between your fingers to make it bend more easily. Do this to all of the strips. You may also roll them with a rolling pin.

2 Roll each cardboard strip lengthwise so that the ends touch. Tape the ends together. Do this to all the strips.

3 Tear your strips of newspaper and mix your flour-and-water paste. (See box.)

Papier-mâché the cardboard rings. Apply paste to the cardboard. One by one, lay strips of paper over the paste-covered area, smoothing them down with more paste. Continue until all the rings are covered with at least three layers of papier-mâché. Allow them to dry.

The rings will not be perfect circles and they will have a good deal of texture. The rings can be slightly flattened into an oval shape while they are still wet. This will help them to lie properly and not tip sideways.

4 OPTIONAL: For a smoother finish, apply a final, single layer of tissue paper in the same manner as papier-mâché. Tissue paper is more difficult to handle than newspaper, as it tends to fall apart when it gets wet. Allow the rings to dry completely.

5 Prime your napkin rings with gesso, a white acrylic primer that will prevent the newsprint from showing through your paint.

Using acrylic paints, paint the rings the color of your choice, taking into consideration what colors your decorations will be.

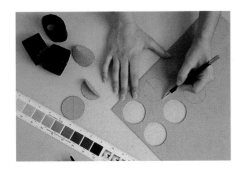

6 Create the decorations of your choice by folding, crumpling and forming newspaper and lightweight cardboard. Tape around your shapes.

Don't make the decorations too big or the napkin rings will tip sideways. Check the size of the decorations as you make them by taping them in place with a napkin in the ring.

7 Papier-mâché over these ornaments, using narrow strips of paper to conform to the small indentations and configurations.

8 Prime the decorations with gesso.

9 Using acrylic paints, paint the decorations in the appropriate colors. Apply a basic color first and then add details.

10 Using carpenter's glue or a hot glue gun, attach the decorations to the rings. For better adhesion, you may wish to rough-up the surfaces to be glued together. This can be done with an emery board or sandpaper. If you use carpenter's glue, tape the parts together until the glue dries.

11 Paint the entire napkin ring with a gloss varnish.

12 Party-time!

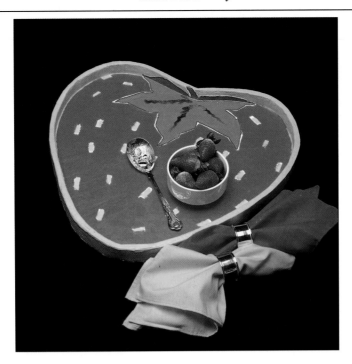

Trays

These trays make wonderful, practical gifts that will be appreciated as an original piece of art, either to be used or hung on a wall.

There is basic carpentry involved in this project. To create the interesting shapes that make these trays unique, the flat area of the tray is cut with a jigsaw or band saw from ¼-inch (0.5 cm) plywood. While many lumberyards will cut down a full sheet of plywood, they will only make straight cuts and won't guarantee accuracy. Have the lumberyard cut a sheet of plywood into 24-inch (61 cm) square pieces. Later you can cut the curved shapes yourself with a jigsaw or band saw. Each of these saws has a narrow, vertical blade and is specifically made for scrolling, while a saw with a circular blade, such as a table saw, will cut only straight lines.

Don't make your tray too large. A surface area equivalent to an 18-inch (46 cm) square or smaller is a good size. The plywood won't withstand a great deal of weight and could be a hazard if overloaded.

Once you are past the carpentry stage, the trays are quite simple to construct and finish. This is a project with a great deal of flexibility. The choices of shape and finishing determine the mood of your tray: romantic, tropical, subdued, bright, country, childlike, and so on. Unless you are a particularly talented artist, try to avoid the temptation to get bogged down in realism in your paint job. The uneven texture of the papier-mâché can be frustrating and the tray's edges may get in your way. The most successful trays are those that are based on general themes like moon and stars, underwater scenes, landscapes or cityscapes, and that are painted in a lively, nonrealistic way.

The following instructions are for the strawberry tray only. The other examples are shown to inspire you. The basic construction is the same for all trays; only the shapes and paint treatments vary. You can expand your options by cutting geometric shapes and working within them. Half-circles are ideal for landscapes and sunsets. Triangles, especially uneven ones, can lend an air of tension and a feeling of jazzy, off-base modernism.

When your tray has been varnished, it will be water-resistant and can be wiped with a damp cloth. It should not be submerged in water or put in the dishwasher.

How to do it

MATERIALS:

Drawing paper and marker

Quarter-inch (0.5 cm) plywood,
 24 x 24 inches (61 x 61 cm)

Jigsaw or band saw

Fine sandpaper

Corrugated cardboard

Ruler

Utility knife

Waxed paper

Hot glue gun and glue sticks

Flour and water

Newspaper

Primer (gesso), acrylic paints
 and brushes

OPTIONAL:

Rolling pin

Varnish

FINISHED SIZE (strawberry tray):

Width at widest point: 19 inches (48 cm)

Height through center: 16 inches (40 cm)

Papier-mâché Basics

NEWSPAPER STRIPS

- Newspaper has a grain. Tear it in the right direction and it will tear straight and evenly.

CLEANUP

- Place a plastic bag in your paste pot for quick cleanup.

PASTE RECIPE

- Add 1½ cups (350 mL) water to 1 cup (250 mL) flour and 2 large spoonfuls of salt. Mix it with your hands.

APPLICATION

- When spreading paste, apply it liberally.
- Do not dip the paper strips in the paste. Lay them on the wet paste area and smooth with more paste.
- Apply at least three layers. Five is preferable.

1 On paper, draw a pattern outlining the shape of your tray. If your design is symmetrical, fold your pattern in half and draw half of the pattern against the fold.

 Cut out your pattern.

2 Open and lay the pattern on a piece of ¼-inch (0.5 cm) plywood. Draw around it.

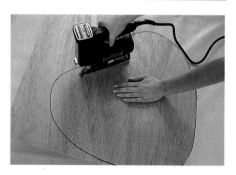

3 Place the plywood on a box or workbench so that the cutting edge is free. Cut along your line with a jigsaw.

 Lightly sand the edges with fine sandpaper.

4 Using a ruler and a utility knife, measure, mark and cut strips of corrugated cardboard 2 inches (5 cm) wide and as long as possible. These are for the edges of your tray and longer pieces mean fewer joins. Double-thickness corrugated cardboard is preferable and can be found in boxes that carry heavy shipments like liquor or books.

 Be certain that the corrugations inside the cardboard run crosswise. When you look at the long edge of a strip, you should see a line of holes.

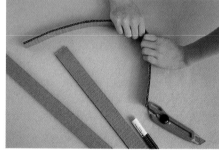

5 Working along the length of the strips, crush them with your fingers so that they bend more readily. You can also roll them with a rolling pin.

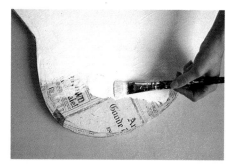

6 Place your plywood cut-out shape on waxed paper on a flat surface. Using a hot glue gun, glue the cardboard strips onto the edge of the plywood. Be certain they are flush with the bottom of the plywood. When one strip ends, glue another one to it and continue until the tray is completely surrounded. Cut and attach the last piece to fit.

7 OPTIONAL: If you wish to reinforce the edges for extra strength, cut a second set of cardboard strips 1¾ inches (4.5 cm) wide. Glue them against the inside of the first edge and the top of the plywood to create a double thickness.

8 Tear your newspaper strips and mix your flour-and-water paste. (See box.)

Start by applying papier-mâché to the cardboard edges. Spread paste onto the cardboard and the adjoining plywood. Lay the end of a strip of paper onto the top of the tray near the edge. Bring it over the edge and around to the bottom of the tray. Smooth it down with paste. Place the next strip partially over the first one and smooth it down with paste. Continue in this overlapping manner until the entire edge has been covered. If the edge becomes soft, allow it to dry before continuing.

Papier-mâché the flat areas, applying paste to the bare plywood. Wet it thoroughly as the moisture tends to soak in. Apply short pieces of paper either at random or in a pattern. Be certain to smooth each piece down with paste. Allow the tray to dry thoroughly.

Test your tray to be certain the edges are stiff and strong. If they are soft or wobbly, apply one or two more layers of papier-mâché. Allow it to dry.

9 Prime your tray with gesso, a white acrylic primer that will prevent the newsprint from showing through your paint.

10 Using acrylic paints, paint your tray with the design you have in mind. (See FINISHING section for ideas.)

A final coat of glossy varnish will make your tray more durable. The somewhat rubbery texture of the varnish, coupled with the slightly uneven papier-mâché surface, will help prevent objects from sliding around on the tray.

11 Breakfast in bed, anyone?

Mermaid

Mermaids are elegant, sensuous and elusive. I wanted this mermaid sculpture to embody all of these qualities and to also look antique, as if she were stolen from the bow of an old sailing ship – weathered, beaten, but still graceful and timeless.

Constructing the mermaid's skeleton is not difficult. She is made from formed, densely crumpled and taped newspaper. But her small size, coupled with a certain amount of realism and detail, make her very challenging. The detail of her face and hands, as well as the relief of the scales and the ribs on the tail, require intricate, sculptural papier-mâché. Patience is your best ally on this project and the results are well worth the effort.

The base in the photo was professionally constructed from acrylic. This sleek, solid, clean-looking base accentuates the sculptural quality of the mermaid by contrasting with her textures and colors.

You can make a wooden base yourself. A stained and finished piece of oak or other good-quality wood can be used. Long wood screws can be screwed in and countersunk from the bottom, to mount and support the mermaid flush to the base.

Another alternative is to create the mermaid as a self-supporting sculpture with a flat area on the bottom as a base. To do this, slice a piece off the bottom with a bread knife after you have applied the papier-mâché. Papier-mâché over the flat area and leave it scale-free.

I created the mermaid with a moon under her arm, the moon being associated not only with mythology but also with sailors' navigation. You can create your mermaid with other props, possibly a string of stars, a sun and moon together, or seashells. Her arms need not be rounded, but can be in whatever position you wish. Be as intricate and fussy as you like with your paint job. The mermaid doesn't have to be antiqued. She can be a brunette or a redhead with pale, glowing skin, iridescent scales and a decorative gown, or olive-skinned with scales in mango, azure and other tropical shades. The choice is yours.

How to do it

MATERIALS:

Newspaper

Masking tape

Utility knife

Flour and water

Foam board or corrugated cardboard
    for hair and tail

Lightweight cardboard for scales

Bread knife or similar knife
    with a long blade

Hot glue gun

Primer (gesso)

Acrylic paints and brushes

OPTIONAL:

Carpenter's glue for paste

Modelling paste and stiff-bristled brush

Base of plastic or wood
    to mount mermaid

FINISHED SIZE:

Height: 19½ inches (49.5 cm)

Width: 19½ inches (49.5 cm)

1 To make the mermaid's body, firmly crumple and roll newspaper to form a large shrimp-like shape. Wrap tape tightly around the newspaper, adding more crumpled paper to fill in depressed areas or to even out the silhouette, as needed. The whole structure should be uniformly dense, firm and sturdy.

2 Crumple newspaper and form the head and neck in one piece. The neck should be extra long in order to insert it into the body. Wrap the head and neck well in tape.

3 To create the mermaid's arms, make two cylinders by tightly twisting a full sheet of newspaper. Then bend it in half and twist it again. Bend the cylinders into the desired shapes and wrap them well in tape. Trim them to the correct length for each arm.

Attach both arms securely to the body with masking tape.

Crumple pieces of paper and tape them in place for breasts and buttocks.

4 Attach the head by cutting a hole in the body with a utility knife. Make the hole small enough that the neck fits snugly into it. Cut the hole to a depth that suits the proportional length of the neck and head when inserted.

5 Insert the neck into the hole. Tape the head securely in place.

Examine your mermaid and adjust any proportions that don't look right – longer or shorter arms, larger or smaller head.

6 Tear your newspaper strips and mix your flour-and-water paste. (See box.)

Apply paste over an area of your mermaid. One by one, lay paper strips over the paste-covered area and smooth them down with more paste. Continue adding and overlapping paper strips until you have applied at least three layers of papier-mâché. Progress over the entire mermaid.

Use narrower paper strips on curved shapes, or make tears in the sides of the strips to make them conform.

7 Create lips, a nose, a brow and fingers by crumpling small pieces of newspaper. Dip them in paste and place them in position. Mold their shape with your fingers.

Papier-mâché over them with narrow strips of paper.

8 Cut out the shape of the hair from a piece of foam board or corrugated cardboard, with an indentation that fits very tightly around the top of the head.

Draw and cut out the tail fins in one piece. These should be symmetrical. Leave a square tab attached to the base of the fins. This tab will be inserted into the tail.

Papier-mâché Basics

NEWSPAPER STRIPS
- **Newspaper has a grain. Tear it in the right direction and it will tear straight and evenly.**

CLEANUP
- **Place a plastic bag in your paste pot for quick cleanup.**
- **Coat your hands with Vaseline for easier paste removal.**

PASTE RECIPE
- **Add 1½ cups (350 mL) water to 1 cup (250 mL) flour. Mix it with your hands.**
- **Add 2 large spoonfuls of salt. Salt will help prevent mold from forming in your paste or on your project.**
- **Add about ¼ cup (50 mL) of carpenter's glue for extra strength (optional).**

APPLICATION
- **When spreading paste, apply it liberally.**
- **Do not dip the paper strips in the paste. Lay each strip on the wet paste area and smooth over with more paste.**
- **Apply at least three layers. Five is preferable.**

DRYING
- **Papier-mâché can take more than one day to dry.**
- **Test your project by touch. If it feels cool, it needs more time to dry.**

9 Using a knife with a long blade like a bread knife, cut sideways across the top of the tail.

10 Slide the tab of the tail fins into the cut in the tail. Tape the tab in position if it is loose.

11 Place the hair-shaped foam board onto the mermaid's head. If it is loose, tape it in position.

12 Working on one side at a time, create hair by crumpling newspaper, dipping it in paste and laying it onto the foam board. Prevent the foam board from bending under the weight of the papier-mâché by supporting it with a box or similar support until the papier-mâché has dried.

Make ribs on the tail fins by rolling paste-soaked newspaper into thin cylinders. Place them on the tail and apply papier-mâché over them.

Allow everything to dry before turning the mermaid over.

13 If you want your mermaid to hold a moon under her arm, make one that fits, from newspaper. Tape it well.

Papier-mâché the moon in position.

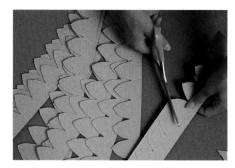

14 Make the mermaid's scales by cutting rows of uniform scales from lightweight cardboard.

15 Using a hot glue gun, attach the scales to the mermaid. Starting at the tail, overlap and offset the scales to the best of your ability. Try to hide joins on the underside of the body. Scoring into the edge of the cardboard opposite the scales helps the cardboard conform to the curve of the body.

You can finish the edge of the scales at waist-level with a belt of cardboard fish.

16 OPTIONAL: Using a stiff-bristled brush, apply modelling paste to the scales. While it is still wet, smooth it with a softer brush dipped in water. This will thicken the scales, add texture and fill holes and crevices.

17 Prime the mermaid with gesso, a white acrylic primer that will prevent newsprint from showing through your paint.

18 Using acrylic paints, paint your mermaid as you have imagined her. (See FINISHING section for ideas and information on creating an antique finish.)

Jennifer

I created this life-sized figure of eight-year-old Jennifer skipping to capture the mood of early spring and to challenge some of the rules of papier-mâché construction. Papier-mâché tends to have a mind of its own and doesn't lend itself to smooth texture, accurate modelling and intricate detail. If you attempt a figure like this, you should have a good knowledge of papier-mâché application. Creating a fairly smooth, realistic figure is time-consuming and demanding. If you find the challenge of fashioning a figure like Jennifer intimidating, you can stick to papier-mâché construction and eliminate the time-consuming smooth finishing and make a cartoon figure instead. To do this, exaggerate the pose and the features to achieve a caricature of, for example, a kid showing off on a skateboard or an ice-cream-dribbling baby.

A person of any age is acceptable as the subject for figure construction. While a child's lack of affectation can be an inspiration, an adult can be created with exaggerated body shapes, as well as interesting wrinkles and features that lend themselves very well to the texture of papier-mâché. Caricatures of famous personalities are excellent subjects, as are clowns, mimes and other theatrical types. When creating a caricature, always make a preliminary sketch or several sketches for reference. Personalities such as movie stars and political figures are more effective if their heads are too large for their bodies, similar to the way editorial cartoonists draw them.

Adults can be created larger or smaller than life and their body proportions can be altered for effect. However, altering body proportions doesn't work for children. Unless a child is created dramatically larger or smaller than life, deviations from normal size and proportions can seem disturbing.

Children have definite growth patterns and proportions. If you opt for realism, it helps to have a human model available who is the right age and sex for comparisons of size and features. If a live model isn't available, take photos and measurements of a person for reference.

Avoid creating a figure that looks like a store mannequin or a dressed-up doll. Your figure should be a piece of sculpture that sets a mood or tells a story rather than simply standing still. Create papier-mâché clothes or make clothes from fabric and paint them instead of dressing your figure in purchased clothes. Not only are purchased clothes nonsculptural, they also require cutting apart and resewing onto the figure. Hair should also be a sculptured part of the figure. You can either form papier-mâché hair or use a wig. Wigs can be expensive and the cheaper ones are very unnatural-looking. If a wig is used, it should be glued and lacquered in place. Every part of the sculpture should be solid and an integral part of the whole.

Jennifer is deliberately balanced on the toes of one foot to make her more interesting and to capture a fleeting moment. In order to support a standing, running or leaping figure, especially one that is cantilevered from one point, an armature must be built and securely fastened to a base of corresponding size. This is also necessary for monsters or dinosaurs that are supported by legs and are top-heavy.

The sculpture of Jennifer shown here is composed of several layers of material: chicken wire, papier-mâché strips, papier-mâché pulp, modelling paste that is sanded smooth and, finally, clothing and paint. Props such as her baseball cap and skipping rope add scale and realism.

The following instructions pertain to Jennifer, but they are meant to guide you in creating your own Bobby or Michael or Sarah, rather than simply duplicating Jennifer.

How to do it

MATERIALS:

Heavy paper

Steel bracket and screws

¾-inch (2 cm) plywood

Strip of perforated metal or
    very heavy wire

Nuts and bolts

Coat hangers or wire of similar weight

Chicken wire

Newspaper

Flour and water

Masking tape

Papier-mâché pulp

Coarse, fine and medium sandpaper

Modelling paste

Gesso

Brush or sponge

Commercial modelling clay

Hot glue

Acrylic paint

OPTIONAL:

Foam board or corrugated cardboard

Carpenter's glue for paste and other uses

Colored pencil

Wig

Baseball cap

Spray lacquer

Buckles

Fabric

Skipping rope

Rubber gloves

FINISHED SIZE:

Height: 51 inches (129.5 cm)

Width: 12 inches (30.5 cm)
        (at shoulders)

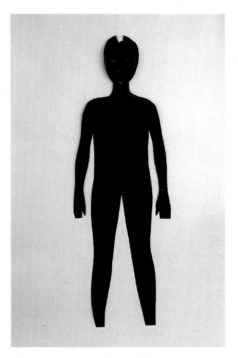

1 To estimate the proportions of your figure, collect reference material and measurements. Draw and cut a life-sized replica from heavy paper.

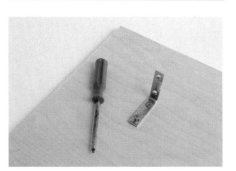

2 For the base, use a piece of ¾-inch (2 cm) plywood; a 2-foot (62 cm) square is a good, stable size. Screw heavy steel brackets where you wish to position the foot or feet. For extra strength you may use more than one bracket for each foot.

3 Create an armature by attaching a strip of perforated steel or very heavy wire to each bracket with nuts and bolts. Wrap it with coat hanger wire or wire of similar weight. Angle the armature to approximate the position of the leg.

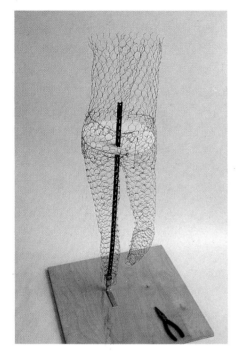

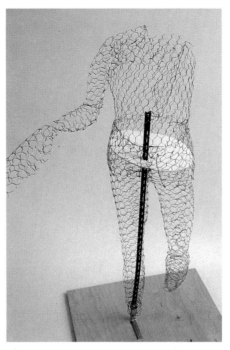

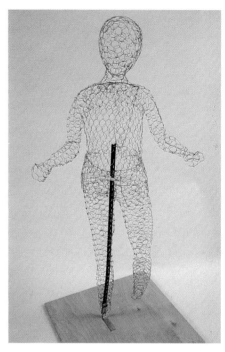

4 Working from the bottom up, form the legs by molding chicken wire around the armature. Leave the feet until later, when the shape and size will be easier to approximate. Continue adding chicken wire to form the hips and abdomen.

To create support and help maintain shape, foam board or cardboard can be inserted into the chicken wire wherever necessary. Coat hanger wire or wire of similar weight can secure the armature to the chicken wire to increase stability.

5 Continue working up the torso, adding and forming the chicken wire. Create arms and shoulders, adding support wires as they are needed.

6 Keep going until the entire body is formed, except for the hands and feet. Leave some excess wire in the area of the hands.

7 Mold the feet from chicken wire.

Inspect the figure and adjust any proportions or shapes. Several layers of various materials will cover the chicken wire structure; at this stage, therefore, your person should be slightly slimmer than you want the final figure to be. If the figure is too fat, compress the chicken wire. If the body is too thin, stretch the wire.

Papier-mâché Basics

NEWSPAPER STRIPS

- Newspaper has a grain. Tear it in the right direction and it will tear straight and evenly.

CLEANUP

- Place a plastic bag in your paste pot for quick cleanup.
- Coat your hands with Vaseline for easier paste removal.

PASTE RECIPE

- Add 1¹/₂ cups (350 mL) water to 1 cup (250 mL) flour. Mix it with your hands.
- Add 2 large spoonfuls of salt. Salt will help prevent mold from forming in your paste or on your project.
- Add about ¹/₄ cup (50 mL) of carpenter's glue for extra strength (optional).

APPLICATION

- When spreading paste, apply it liberally.
- Do not dip the paper strips in the paste. Lay each strip on the wet paste area and smooth over with more paste.
- Apply at least three layers. Five is preferable.

DRYING

- Papier-mâché can take more than one day to dry.
- Test your project by touch. If it feels cool, it needs more time to dry.

8 Tear newspaper strips and mix some paste. (See box.) Working from the bottom up, apply several layers of papier-mâché to the chicken wire. If it is difficult to get the papier-mâché to stick, apply random strips of masking tape to the chicken wire first. For your first layer, dip the paper strips into the paste first. (See box for application of subsequent layers.)

9 Continue until the entire torso, arms and legs are covered. Examine proportions as you go. If necessary, remove papier-mâché to alter the chicken wire. Then reapply papier-mâché, as needed. Apply three to five layers.

10 Papier-mâché over the head and face. Allow it to dry. Begin adding shape to the face and the rest of the figure with crumpled paper. Tape the paper well with masking tape. Jennifer now looks as though she has had the misfortune of being in an accident.

11 Jennifer makes a quick recovery as the taped, crumpled paper additions are covered in more papier-mâché.

If you prefer a handcrafted-looking figure rather than a realistic-looking one, continue working with papier-mâché, molding ears, teeth and facial features until you are satisfied with the results. Papier-mâché the hands, feet and any other areas you wish to complete and move on to the finishing of the figure. (See step 22.)

12 Using either gray or white papier-mâché pulp (see FINISHING section, page 129 for more information), apply a thin layer over the entire figure. Try to eliminate hand imprints and keep the layer of pulp as smooth as possible. Form can be molded from the pulp as you apply it. Allow it to dry.

13 The rough finish of the pulp can be left, if you like the effect. It can be painted a solid color, or perhaps faux bronze or stone. For a smoother finish, sand the pulp to remove rough texture using a medium to coarse sandpaper. This will not produce a completely smooth finish but it will remove the obvious bumps.

14 To fill in the uneven texture of the pulp, apply modelling paste or a mixture of modelling paste and gesso, a white acrylic primer. Use a brush or sponge.

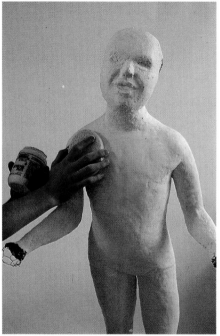

15 Apply several layers of modelling paste, smoothing each layer with a damp sponge. Sand with medium to fine sandpaper after each layer is dry.

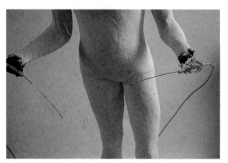

16 Thread a wire through the skipping rope to give it extra solidity and to retain its position when bent. It should then be positioned in Jennifer's hands.

17 Mold the hands and feet from papier-mâché pulp. Pay special attention to size and position. A common error is to put the thumbs on the wrong sides of the hands!

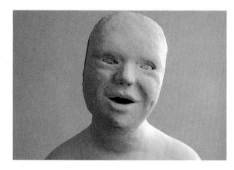

18 Carve, add and form the facial features.

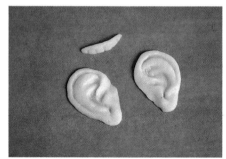

19 Form the ears and teeth from commercial modelling clay.

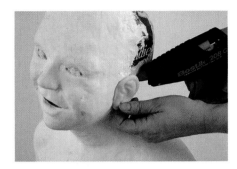

20 Attach the ears with hot glue. Continue adding modelling paste and sanding it, filling in minor depressions and craters.

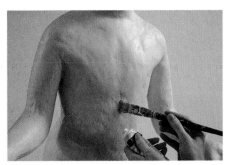

22 Prime your figure. (See box.) To achieve fairly lifelike skin tones, layer several thin coats of the same family of color, for example, an orange-toned base coat followed by pale pink, followed by off-white, until you have the color balance you desire.

24 Add hair in the form of papier-mâché or a wig. Jennifer wears a baseball cap with hair showing only on the sides. To achieve this, cut a wig into sections to be glued selectively in place.

If you want the hair to maintain a certain position, parts of the wig can be attached to pieces of cardboard with carpenter's glue. Spray lacquer will also keep the hair in position. This should be applied last (see step 35), when all construction and painting is complete.

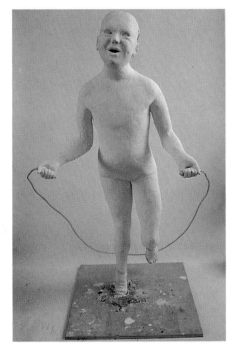

21 Coat the hands and feet with modelling paste and sand it smooth. Inspect your figure. Fill and sand any indentations or irregularities until you are completely satisfied.

23 Eyes, eyelashes and freckles can be executed with a combination of paint and colored pencil. If you want the eyes to be realistic, avoid "floating" eyeballs and irises that have spokes drawn onto them. Take a softer approach by adding some shadow under the eyelid and around the rim of the iris. Avoid drawing individual eyelashes. A smudged look is more convincing.

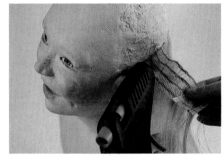

25 Attach the wig or pieces of the wig onto the head, using hot glue.

26 If your figure is life-sized, various accessories can be added: belts, buckles, bracelets, rings, scarves and, in this case, Jennifer's baseball cap. (The brim was cut back and the hat was primed with gesso and glued in place.)

27 Clothing can be constructed from papier-mâché or formed from fabric.

To make fabric clothing, cut cotton sheeting or a similar fabric into the required shapes. A knowledge of sewing is helpful here!

Turn the edges under, clipping curves, and secure the edges with carpenter's glue.

28 Position the clothing onto the figure, taping it in place. Glue seams together and tape them until they are dry.

29 A structured form, such as a gathered waist, can be taped in position.

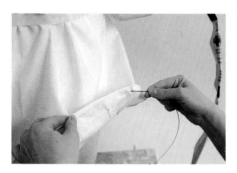

30 Wire threaded through hems can be bent in position to give the clothes the illusion of movement.

31 Mix carpenter's glue with water to achieve a sloppy consistency. Using a brush, saturate the fabric with the mixture. Form, support and secure the fabric as you go to give it an exaggerated impression of movement. Be as theatrical as you wish. Allow it to dry, then remove any tape or props. If the fabric isn't stiff enough to maintain its position, apply another coat of the glue mixture.

34 Paint the shoes or sandals, gluing real shoelaces or buckles in place if you wish.

32 Prime the clothing with gesso. When it has dried, paint it in the color or design of your choice. Try not to overpower the figure with vivid colors or patterns. Most kids like to wear solid colors, large patterns, or one message or emblem on their chests. Tiny patterns tend to look like pyjamas. For repetitive designs, stencilling may be the best method of execution.

35 If a wig is used, lacquer the hair to keep it in position. Use clear, fast-drying spray lacquer. Wear rubber gloves and support the hair as it dries.

33 If you like, add items such as pockets or collars to the clothes. Jennifer's bow is threaded with wire and glued in place to defy gravity.

36 Cover the base with a surface appropriate to your subject. Papier-mâché pulp was used for Jennifer because it most closely resembles concrete. Paw prints were impressed as a finishing touch.

37 Remind Jennifer that there's no skipping allowed in the house.

Finishing

Now comes the fun – the metamorphosis of your project from a gray lump to something spectacular. This section discusses surface texturing, painting and decorating, to give you ideas and inspiration. Some finishing techniques are better suited to certain types of projects. Leaf through the following pages and find the look and the application that you consider most appropriate to your project and to your abilities.

Textured surface finishes should be applied first; then you can prime or paint your project. Most other finishing techniques require your project to be primed *before* you apply them. Read the "Basic Paint Job" portion on page 130 before you begin painting. This explains most of the materials you will need and how to use them. Once you are acquainted with the basics, you can move on to more complicated techniques and treatments.

You can treat your project as a canvas to showcase your painterly abilities, or you can use your paint job to accent your three-dimensional object. Remember that you don't have to be a great artist to create an effective design with bold color, splatter or sponge techniques.

Finishing and treatments for papier-mâché objects are almost unlimited, so don't be afraid to experiment and try something new. Unexpected designs and color combinations can spell the difference between the pedestrian and the extraordinary.

Surface Texture

SANDPAPER

If you prefer a smoother surface on your object, it can be lightly sanded. Medium to fine sandpaper can be used, depending upon the thickness of your papier-mâché coverage. An emery board is good for small objects and tight corners or indentations. Sanding will remove small lumps of glue, wrinkles and some high spots.

It isn't appropriate for achieving total smoothness because of the fragility of the surface and the ease with which it can be worn through. Rather than sanding the papier-mâché directly, coat the object in papier-mâché pulp or modelling paste and then sand it.

The usual texture of papier-mâché that has been applied with paper strips and paste is hard and fairly lumpy. In most cases, this is desirable. However, occasionally there is a need for either a smoother, more wrinkled or more distressed surface. The following examples explain how to achieve different textures.

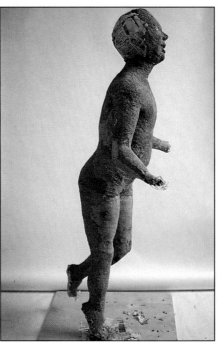

PAPIER-MACHE PULP

This medium is available at hobby stores in blocks of various weights, colored either white or gray. If you use the white pulp for finishing, your project won't need priming. The pulp is usually inpregnated with dry paste; add water, according to the directions, to produce a pulpy material. This can be spread over your object in a thin coating and allowed to dry. When dry, it is extremely hard and durable.

For a smooth finish, knead the pulp well and spread it carefully, eliminating finger depressions as you go. When dry, sand the surface with medium-grade sandpaper.

To create texture – for a monster's porous-looking skin or to give a piece of sculpture a cast-bronze appearance – add extra water to the pulp and apply it loosely without too much smoothing. It will have the appearance of pitted concrete.

Once the pulp has completely dried, it can be painted or left as is.

MODELLING PASTE

This is a thick, liquid acrylic substance that dries to a very hard and durable consistency. It can be applied with sponges or by brush to the surface of an object. This material has the appearance and texture of plaster but is less prone to cracking and breaking.

For a smooth surface, apply it with an almost-dry sponge, working it into crevices and filling hollows. After allowing it to set for a few minutes, smooth it with a damp sponge or your hands. If this finish isn't flawless enough for your taste, sand it after it has dried, and repeat the procedure.

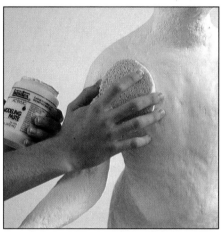

Designs can be etched into modelling paste. Apply a heavy layer, allow it to set for several minutes, and then carve or imprint your pattern into the paste.

CLOTH MACHE

For a strong, wrinkly or smooth surface texture, apply the final layer of mâché using strips of fabric. When the surface is painted, the paint will pool in the creases and accentuate the texture. Woven fabrics with cotton content are best. Woolly, fluffy or knit fabrics are unsuitable.

Use either flour-and-water paste (see recipe, page 16) or wallpaper paste. Tear your fabric into strips about 3 inches (7.5 cm) wide and apply cloth mâché as follows.

How to do it

1 Unlike in papier-mâché application, dip the fabric strips into your paste mixture. Saturate the fabric. Then draw the strip between your fingers to eliminate the excess paste.

2 Lay the strips on your object, smoothing or wrinkling them as much as you wish. Allow the object to dry.

The Basic Paint Job

MATERIALS

BRUSHES:
Purchase brushes that are compatible in size with the area you are painting. Virtually any type of brush is suitable. There are brushes on the market made specifically for acrylic paint; however, I've never found it a problem to use other types.

You will probably need one large and one medium-sized square-tipped brush for priming and general paint application, as well as small square-tipped and one small, pointed brush for detailed work.

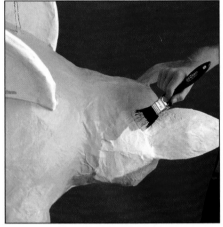

The materials described in this section and the directions for the basic paint job are appropriate to all projects.

Most acrylic paints can be purchased premixed to the correct color. When mixing colors yourself, experiment with a small amount first to avoid discarding large quantities of expensive paint. Remember that adding black or white to a color will change the property of a color rather than lightening or darkening it.

When laying down a flat color, check the label on the paint for opacity. For a flat, dense color, use opaque paints. Use transparent or semitransparent paints for a glaze of color.

SETUP

When painting, place your object on plastic or clean white paper. Don't use newspaper because the ink will transfer onto your paint job. Have a jar or cup of water handy for rinsing brushes, and rags or paper towels to remove excess water from brushes. Change water frequently to prevent it from dirtying your paint. If you need to mix quantities of paint, use plastic yogurt, margarine or dairy product containers, especially if they have lids for storage, which will prevent the paint from drying. A piece of plastic or nonporous cardboard can act as a palette for small quantities of paint.

Medium-priced brushes are best. Cheap ones will shed hairs and their coarse fibers will leave wiry marks in your paint. The high-quality hairs in expensive brushes will be damaged by the aggressive brushwork required on the uneven texture of the papier-mâché.

Always wash your brushes thoroughly with soap and water immediately after using them. Once acrylic paint has dried into a brush, no amount of soaking will remove it.

PRIMER:

Prime your project before you paint it. Use acrylic primer, also known as gesso. Gesso is compatible with the acrylic paints that you will be using for your paint job. It is a thick white primer used by artists to prime canvasses. Gesso will prevent the newsprint from showing through your paint and its consistency will fill any small creases or indentations that you'd like to hide.

If you wish to avoid the priming stage, you can use plain newsprint for your final papier-mâché layer. (By the way, why is the daily paper, with printing on it, called news*paper*, while plain paper, without printing on it, is called news*print*? Why do we drive on the parkway and park on the driveway?)

PAINTS:

Always use acrylic paints, which are water-based for easy mixing, simple cleanup and fast drying. They come in a full range of premixed colors in both jars and tubes and are permanent, lightfast and flexible. Acrylics are also water-resistant when dry and are compatible with many other acrylic products, including, varnishes, primer and compounds such as modelling paste.

Read the label on the paint container for advice on transparency, opacity and any toxicity warnings regarding that particular brand.

VARNISHES:

Use acrylic glossy or matte varnishes to add richness to your paint job or to give it added protection. These varnishes are also called "mediums" because they can be used as extenders for acrylic paint.

Matte medium has a low-lustre sheen and is ideal for general use. Gloss medium can be applied to eyes, teeth, etc. for a wet look or to enrich color, especially on items like the Napkin Rings (page 102) or the Trays (page 106) that are designed for the kitchen or associated with food. Gloss finishes accentuate texture. If you wish to downplay unevenness of texture, use only matte medium finishes.

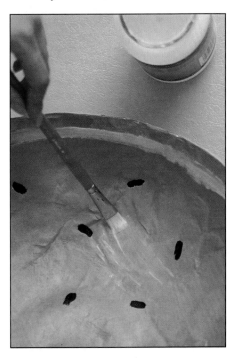

Items finished with acrylic paint and protected with varnish are water-resistant, which means they can be wiped with a damp cloth and will withstand a spill. They should not be submerged in water or put in the dishwasher.

How to do it

1 Select a premixed color or mix your own shade. Mix enough for at least two coats, since it is difficult to match a custom-mixed color if you run out partway through your paint application. If you do run out, apply a full coat of the new color.

Apply a smooth, even coat of paint over your primed object. Allow it to dry. Apply additional coats until the coverage is dense, smooth and solid.

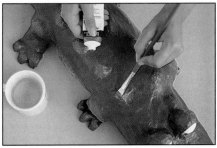

2 Add highlights in a similar color or in white.

Painting Realism

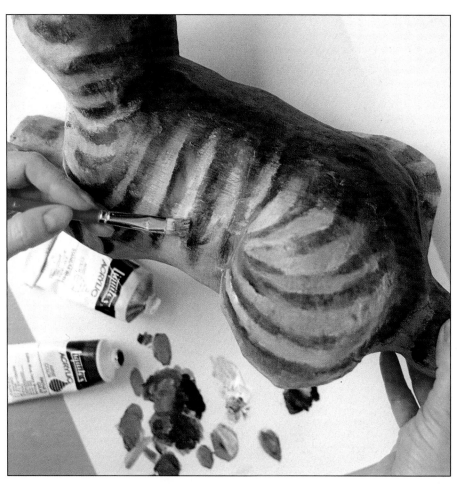

THE HUMAN FIGURE

To achieve fairly lifelike skin tones, prime your figure with gesso, then layer several thin coats of the same family of color, for example, an orange-toned base coat followed by pale pink, followed by off-white, until you have the color balance you desire. Allow each previous color to "glow" through the next. This will create depth of color.

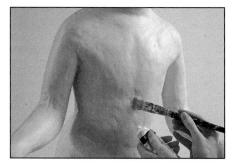

Eyes, eyelashes and freckles can be executed with a combination of paint and colored pencil. If you want the eyes to be fairly realistic, avoid "floating" eyeballs and irises that have spokes drawn onto them. Take a softer approach by adding some shadow under the eyelid and around the rim of the iris. Avoid drawing individual eyelashes. A smudged look is more convincing.

Creating realism depends on the artist's powers of observation and duplication. Even an unreal object like Refrigerator Raider (page 82) can include a bit of realism for effect – in the food that he holds, his lizard-like skin and the gleam in his eye.

Because your object is already three-dimensional, some of the requirements for creating realism, such as proportion, perspective and content, are already taken care of. References can be helpful when painting a pattern such as a tabby cat's stripes or for color matching. But guard against becoming a slave

to your reference material, especially photos. No paint job is going to be true-to-life because the object being painted doesn't look completely real; it does not have absolutely realistic proportions or texture. Proceed with this in mind to avoid frustration.

The following instructions are for painting a human figure and a realistic dog (The Mutt project, page 38). They are meant to be an example of how to achieve a certain degree of realism. Adapt the instructions as necessary to suit your project.

How to do it

PALETTE:
Burnt sienna, burnt umber (medium and dark brown), titanium white, pink, black.

OPTIONAL: Raw sienna, raw umber (more browns), unbleached titanium (beige), red or deep pink.

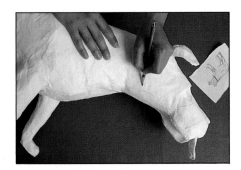

1 When the primer is completely dry, draw the general patterns on your dog with a pencil.

2 Fill in the brown areas with a coat of burnt sienna.

3 Starting at the center of the brown areas, apply burnt umber, working it out to the edges and blending it into the base coat. Add more burnt sienna to the edges for blending, if necessary. Highlight or darken all brown areas to create depth.

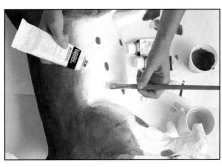

4 Apply titanium white to areas that you wish to be pure white. Add some beige to areas that you wish to be more toned down, not bright white.

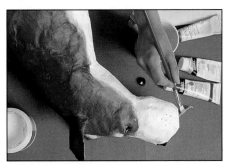

5 Paint the tongue and the insides of the ears pink. Accentuate the center of the tongue with a deeper pink and blend it out to the sides. Paint the nose black.

6 Paint the eyes, or use buttons or modelling clay to create eyes, and glue them in place.

7 Apply gloss varnish to the nose and tongue.

Graphic Painting

In art, the terms for types of painting and techniques of application become redefined over time. In the 1960s and 1970s, "graphic" painting referred to hard-edged paintings and designs in contrasting, even vibrating color combinations. These favored geometric shapes, particularly circles and rainbow stripes.

Today "graphic" refers to a far looser treatment, painterly in texture, executed with unexpected color combinations and tension in the design.

Try to resist the urge to butt colors evenly and uniformly together. The contemporary approach to painting is freewheeling and individual, which perfectly complements the properties of papier-mâché. Keeping your approach casual ensures that any uneven, thin spots aren't considered errors if there is an overall, hand-crafted look. This is in keeping with the uneven texture of papier-mâché .

The following instructions are for the "fish" bowl (Bowls project, page 92), which has a Matisse-like feeling. Adapt the instructions to fit your individual project.

In general, when painting with a combination of opaque and transparent colors, paint the transparent washes first, so that any errors can be covered with the denser colors when they are applied.

How to do it

PALETTE:
Pthalocyanine green (deep turquoise green), titanium white, pthalocyanine blue (deep turquoise blue), indo orange red, Turner's yellow.

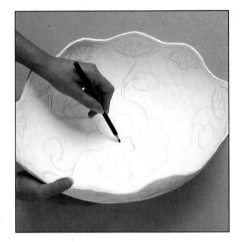

1 When the primer is dry, draw your design with a pencil.

2 Mix pthalocyanine green and white and paint the leaves this color.

3 Add lines for shading and definition with unmixed pthalocyanine green.

4 Thin the pthalocyanine blue with water and paint the background. It will be uneven and transparent.

5 Paint the fish indo orange red, a good contrasting color for the blue and green.

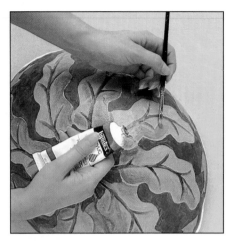

6 Touch up, shade or blend any areas as you wish.

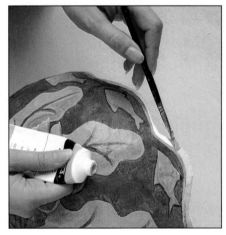

7 Paint the border with Turner's yellow.

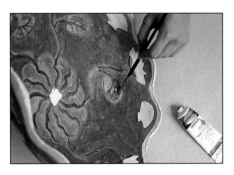

8 Paint the inside of your bowl in a similar fashion.

Special Techniques

Special techniques can produce big results with only a little talent. When working with these methods, remember that the object is to impress the viewer.

When choosing a color scheme, emphasize it. You can go with bold energetic colors, with fresh white and primaries, or with ultra-soft pastels. Drama can also be achieved by using moody, dense blacks with rich accents or decorative Victorian designs.

In addition to the techniques featured here, you can investigate stencilling, stipple painting, string painting (where you dip string into paint and snap it onto, or drag it across your object), or a variety of textural treatments that can be achieved by mixing sand, seeds, etc. into your gesso before painting.

The following instructions are for the objects featured in the photographs. Adapt and change the instructions to suit your project.

ANTIQUING

The crinkly texture of papier-mâché lends itself well to antiquing. Apply your paint with brushes and wipe off areas with rags or sponges, working colors over each other until you have the effect you desire. If you are timid about this technique, go slowly and apply over-coats sparingly. Take time to scrutinize your project before proceeding and strengthen layers by adding more paint if required.

Choose antique colors: forest green, burgundy, yellow ochre, slate blue and gray, as well as dusty colors in blue, rose and green. Metallic accents can also add an air of authenticity.

The following instructions are for the Mermaid (page 110). Alter the colors and applications for your particular object.

How to do it

PALETTE:
Payne's gray (deep blue gray), pthalocyanine blue (deep turquoise blue), unbleached titanium (beige), rose red, titanium white, pink, bronze yellow, metallic gold and bronze.

1 Thin the Payne's gray with water and apply a wash to the entire mermaid. The paint will settle naturally into dents and creases. Allow it to dry.

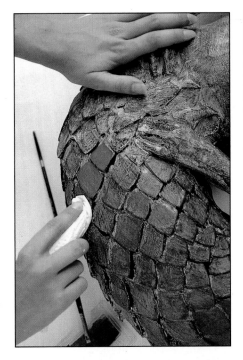

2 Using an almost-dry brush and pthalocyanine blue mixed with a small quantity of unbleached titanium, apply a layer to the high parts of the scales, leaving the deepest crevices gray. With a cloth, blot the paint from the tips of the scales to achieve a glazed appearance in these areas.

3 Work over the mermaid's bodice with rose red, and her hair and moon with bronze yellow, laying down and lifting paint until the color is the desired intensity.

4 Continue, working over her skin with a mixture of white and unbleached titanium, overlaying it with pink where desired.

To complete the antique look, add some "dust" in corners and crevices with unbleached titanium. Work this into the crevices and wipe any excess off the surrounding raised areas.

5 Using a pointed brush, paint the details of the mermaid's face with Payne's gray.

Add any metallic details to her bodice, hair and moon, using the metallic bronze and gold.

SPLATTER

Splatter painting was first introduced to the public in the 1960s by painter Jackson Pollock. While it was shocking then, it is fresh, textural and fascinating to look at now. This is a fun but messy method of painting. Prepare your work area in advance. The drips and splatters can end up in some distant, unexpected areas!

How to do it

1 Choose your colors before you begin: a base-coat color and several colors for splattering. The most successful combinations usually consist of several similar colors, soft pastels, neutrals, or several shades of the same color. Add one or two accent colors to these groups for zest.

Paint your bowl with your chosen color, either a basic color or an accent color. Allow it to dry thoroughly.

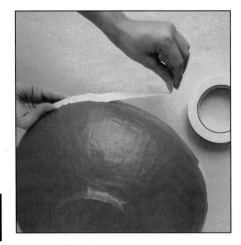

2 Cover your surrounding work area with plastic or paper. Using masking tape, cover any areas on your bowl that you don't want splattered.

3 Mix and thin your paints to the correct consistency, which is like heavy cream. Using a brush with long, soft bristles, saturate it with paint. I found that the best results were achieved by holding the brush loosely in one hand and rapping the handle of it against the other hand. Test your splatter technique on paper first. Then, one by one, splatter each color onto the bowl, turning it to achieve even coverage. Apply the accent colors last.

4 A hair dryer can be used to speed the drying time of each application and to prevent the splatters from running.

Blobs and splashes can add more dimension to the overall effect.

5 Remove the masking tape and make any touchups that you wish. The bowl can be painted with a coat of matte or gloss acrylic varnish.

SPONGE PAINTING

Painting with sponges or rags to layer color can create depth of color, cloud-shapes, "marbling," or soft edges.

Sponge painting is difficult to control and usually takes some trial and error before satisfactory results are achieved. Good results often come under the "happy accident" category.

How to do it

1 Choose a palette of similar colors, either bright shades, as used for Birdo (page 46), dark, dramatic colors or soft shades, as used for the bowl shown here. Apply a base coat of one of the colors. Thin the remaining shades slightly.

2 Using a damp sponge or a rag, layer the colors, sponging away excess paint or adding heavier layers.

3 Continue layering color until you achieve the desired effect.

Découpage

Découpage is the art of decorating objects with cut-out paper images. Often you will see découpage used on furniture or boxes. It is usually heavily varnished to prevent wear.

Découpage is a fast and rewarding way to achieve the appearance of a lush, finely detailed, decorative paint job without the painstaking effort.

1 Choose a printed design that will suit the size of your project and conform to any hills or valleys. Wrapping paper is ideal for découpage because it is thin, the designs are repetitive and it is readily available.

Paint your bowl a solid background color. If you can match your bowl color to the paper background color, you will save yourself a lot of tedious cutting-out time.

3 Mix either a small quantity of wallpaper paste or add some carpenter's glue to water, about half-and-half.

Apply glue to the back of one cutout.

2 Cut out several designs from your paper and position them on your bowl, securing them temporarily with tape. Move them around until you find the best position for each cutout.

4 Carefully place the cutout into position on the bowl, smoothing it with your fingers. Excess paste or glue can be wiped off with a damp cloth or sponge. Apply the other cutouts in the same manner. Allow them to dry.

Apply at least one coat of acrylic varnish.

WALLPAPER DECOUPAGE

Découpage can also be applied using prepasted wallpaper. Border prints are the ideal size for decorating medium-sized projects, especially for that Victorian look.

While wallpaper découpage is somewhat easier to create than découpage using printed paper, it is thicker and the cut edges tend to show more.

How to do it

1 Paint your project a background color, preferably one that will blend with the background of the wallpaper. Cut out and position your designs.

2 One by one, dip the cutouts into water, then apply them to your project, smoothing them with your fingers. Allow it to dry.
Apply at least one coat of varnish.

COMPLETE COVERAGE

Another form of découpage which can be very effective is the complete coverage of your object with cut-out paper images or with fabric. When using this technique, try to develop a theme, for example: crazy headlines from the tabloids ("Hairy Mother Has Wolf Baby!"), hearts, flowers and cherubs from Valentine's Day wrapping paper, calico prints and lace for a Victorian feeling, or comic strips for a zany effect.

How to do it

1 Priming is not necessary when you use this technique. Cut out enough material to completely cover your project.

2 Mix a small quantity of wallpaper paste. One by one, dip the paper or fabric pieces in the paste and lay them onto your project. Be certain all areas of papier-mâché are covered. Remove any excess paste with a damp sponge or rag. Do not rub too hard as the ink on your découpage may smear. Allow the découpage to dry thoroughly and apply at least one coat of varnish.

3-D Additions

If you carve a tight-fitting hole into your papier-mâché and glue the modelling clay item into it, it will be far stronger than if you glue it to the surface. Attach your modelling clay items with carpenter's glue or a hot glue gun.

Carpenter's glue is available in a plastic squeeze bottle with a nozzle for easy application. Tape the items in place while the glue dries. Carpenter's glue can be cleaned up easily when it's wet, but once it's dry, you may need dynamite.

A hot glue gun guarantees fast, strong attachment of small items. *However, hot glue can burn and when it comes in contact with skin it sticks and keeps burning. Children should never use hot glue when unsupervised.*

Homemade Clay Recipe

- In a medium-sized mixing bowl, combine 1$\frac{1}{2}$ cups (350 mL) all-purpose flour with $\frac{1}{2}$ cup (100 mL) cornstarch.

- In a separate bowl mix together $\frac{1}{4}$ cup (50 mL) salt and $\frac{3}{4}$ cup (200 mL) hot water.

- Add the salt water to the dry ingredients. Mix them with a spoon. The particles should stick together.

- Knead the dough for 5 to 10 minutes until it is smooth and elastic.

- Form the shapes that you wish. Bake them on an ungreased cookie sheet in a 200ºF (100ºC) oven. Small and thin items take about 2 hours to bake, while larger pieces can take as long as 4 hours. It's a good idea to set a timer or and alarm clock. If the baker's clay is overcooked, it can become brittle.

Three-dimensional additions add polish and realism to your project. They include items that are modelled from clay, such as teeth, toenails and eyes for creatures, and decorative items such as feathers, ribbon, seeds or fur for a variety of requirements.

Some items need to be attached before the project is painted so that they are included in the application of papier-mâché or the final paint job. Others should be attached later, either because they will obstruct the painting process or because they do not require any paint themselves. The following are guidelines for making and attaching whichever finishing touches best suit your project.

MODELLING CLAY

Modelling clay is useful for small items such as teeth, eyes and toenails for monsters or other beasts. Larger finishing touches that you want to model yourself can be made from papier-mâché. When making items from modelling clay, always choose a clay that will dry or bake to a hard, durable consistency. Either buy a good commercial brand or make it yourself.

FOOD

Thoroughly clean food containers and certain seeds and spices such as sesame seeds can save a great deal of work and add realism to a project because of their true-to-life scale and color. Under no circumstances should perishable food be used.

Fairly realistic food can be formed from papier-mâché or modelling clay and then painted lifelike colors.

Other materials such as foam rubber, styrofoam, carpenter's glue, etc., can be used to create special effects. In the bottom photo, Mozzarella cheese is formed from hot glue.

SEWING TRIMS

Real feathers were attached with hot glue to Pigasus and Birdo. Lace was added to the panties paperweight. Black buttons were used as eyes on The Mutt and self-adhesive Velcro dots were added to the caterpillar paperweight for spots.

Various sewing items can be used for either conventional or unorthodox treatments. Generally, these items must be attached at the very end of the project in order to avoid any contact with wet paint.

You may wish to varnish some of these decorations. Always do a preliminary test before varnishing to guard against color or texture changes.

HAIR

Like clothing, hair should be an integral part of any papier-mâché human figure. It can be created from papier-mâché or a wig may be used. If you use a wig, glue it to the head of your figure with hot glue. It should be soaked with a mixture of carpenter's glue and water or sprayed with clear lacquer and held in position until dry to make it stiff and immobile. A wig can also be cut apart and glued selectively in place, especially if part of the head is to be covered with a hat.

For clown or monster hair, nylon or hemp rope can be glued into sockets and left in tufts or frayed for a fuzzy effect.

CLOTHING

Clothing should be an integral part of your sculpture. Avoid creating a figure that looks like a store mannequin or a dressed-up doll by molding the clothing from papier-mâché or forming it from fabric which is stiffened by soaking it with a glue mixture.

How to do it

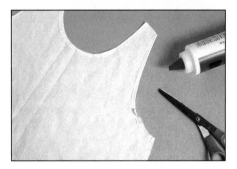

1 To make fabric clothing, cut cotton sheeting or a similar fabric into the required shapes. A knowledge of sewing is helpful here!
Turn the edges under, clipping curves, and secure the edges with carpenter's glue.

2 Position the clothing onto the figure, taping it in place. Glue seams together and tape them until they are dry.

3 A structured form, such as a gathered waist, can be taped in position.

4 Wire threaded through hems can be bent in position to give the clothes the illusion of movement.

5 Mix carpenter's glue with water to achieve a sloppy consistency. Using a brush, saturate the fabric with the mixture. Form, support and secure the fabric as you go to give it an exaggerated impression of movement. Be as theatrical as you wish. Allow it to dry, then remove any tape or props. If the fabric isn't stiff enough to maintain its position, apply another coat of the glue mixture.

6 Prime the clothing with gesso. When it has dried, paint it in the color or design of your choice. Try not to overpower the figure with vivid colors or busy patterns. Tiny patterns tend to look like pyjamas. For repetitive designs, stencilling may be the best method of execution.

7 If you like, add items such as pockets or collars to the clothes. Jennifer's bow is threaded with wire and glued in place to defy gravity.